"Art is perhaps the most powerful means of creating an awareness of the absurdity of our condition. Yet, attempts to relate absurdist philosophy to actual works of art have so far been rare. Shai Tubali's *Cosmos and Camus: Science Fiction Film and the Absurd* provides a model of how to fill this void. The book's first part develops an interpretation of Camus' theory of the absurd. Then Tubali skillfully analyzes four science-fiction films in light of this theory. The resulting considerations will not only increase readers' understanding of these films but also of Camus' philosophy and of our place in the universe."

– Thomas Pölzler, Department of Philosophy, University of Graz,
author of *Moral Reality and the Empirical Sciences*

"Tubali's fascinating book explores the relevance of Albert Camus' philosophy of the absurd to cinematic science fiction – a connection that has regrettably been largely neglected within both Camus scholarship and philosophy of film until now. Tubali homes in on Camus' claim that works of art are valuable mediums for communicating philosophical problems, demonstrating persuasively that sci-fi, in its ability to hold a mirror up to humanity, effectively communicates 'the feeling of the absurd' (which was, as Sartre suggested, Camus' own aim in writing *L'Étranger*). Unpacking, as it does, yet another dimension of Camus' literary-philosophical venture, this insightful book represents a substantial contribution to the literature, and I personally hope to see more of its kind."

– Dr Grace Whistler, author of *Camus' Literary Ethics: Between Form and Content*
and "The Absurd" in *Brill's Companion to Camus*

"The intersections of film and philosophy have long been the subject of a rich, interdisciplinary academic literature, which has recently seen explosive growth. *Cosmos and Camus* is one of the most impressive contributions to this field that I have read in years. After a highly systematic and engagingly written exposition of Camus' work on the absurd, the book offers strikingly original and compelling interpretations of four science fiction films. *Cosmos and Camus* explores the many ways in which philosophy and films can illuminate the human condition and each other."

– Peter Krämer, Senior Research Fellow in Cinema & TV
in the Leicester Media School at De Montfort University, Leicester (UK),
and author of BFI Film Classics on *2001: A Space Odyssey* and *Dr. Strangelove*

Cosmos and Camus

PETER LANG
PROMPT

PETER LANG

Oxford • Bern • Berlin • Bruxelles • New York • Wien

Shai Tubali

Cosmos and Camus

Science Fiction Film and the Absurd

PETER LANG
Oxford • Bern • Berlin • Bruxelles • New York • Wien

Bibliographic information published by **Die Deutsche Nationalbibliothek**.
Die Deutsche Nationalbibliothek lists this publication in the "Deutsche
Nationalbibliografie"; detailed bibliographic data are available
on the Internet at http://dnb.d-nb.de/.

A catalogue record for this book is available from the British Library.

Library of Congress Cataloging-in-Publication Data
Names: Tubali, Shy, author.
Title: Cosmos and Camus : science fiction film and the absurd / Shai Tubali.
Description: Oxford ; New York : Peter Lang, 2020. | Includes
bibliographical references and index. |
Identifiers: LCCN 2020004410 (print) | LCCN 2020004411 (ebook) | ISBN
9781789976649 (paperback) | ISBN 9781789976656 (ebook) | ISBN
9781789976663 (epub) | ISBN 9781789976670 (mobi)
Subjects: LCSH: Science fiction films--History and criticism. | Camus,
Albert, 1913-1960--Criticism and interpretation. | Absurd (Philosophy)
in literature.
Classification: LCC PN1995.9.S26 T83 2020 (print) | LCC PN1995.9.S26
(ebook) | DDC 791.43/615--dc23
LC record available at https://lccn.loc.gov/2020004410
LC ebook record available at https://lccn.loc.gov/2020004411

ISBN 978-1-78997-664-9 (print) • ISBN 978-1-78997-665-6 (epDF)
ISBN 978-1-78997-666-3 (ePub) • ISBN 978-1-78997-667-0 (mobi)

© Peter Lang AG 2020
Published by Peter Lang Ltd, International Academic Publishers, 52 St Giles,
Oxford, OX1 3LU, United Kingdom
oxford@peterlang.com, www.peterlang.com

Contents

Acknowledgments

I wish to express my deepest gratitude to Dr. Mikel Burley and Dr. Stefan Skrimshire from the University of Leeds, who supervised the research that inspired the writing of this book. Together we traversed this uncharted territory, and I cannot imagine attaining any of the insights in this book without our fervent dialogue and their unwavering trust, engagement, and affection.

I am also grateful for the outstanding support that I received from my editor at Peter Lang, Dr. Laurel Plapp. From beginning to end, in difficulty and triumph, she was fully and keenly devoted, as if this were the only book in the world for her.

It is important to acknowledge the scholars who eagerly read the manuscript and strongly endorsed its publication: Dr. David Sorfa, Professor Jacob Golomb, Dr. Peter Krämer, Dr. Grace Whistler, and Dr. Thomas Pölzler. No doubt, the fact that scholars from different fields – Camus Studies, Film Studies, and the Philosophy of Film - expressed interest in this book says much about the unusual interdisciplinary dialogue it evokes.

I would also like to extend my gratitude to Dr. Peter Francev, chief-editor of *Journal of Camus Studies*, and to Dr. Rob Van Gerwen, chief-editor of *Aesthetic Investigations*, for welcoming versions of chapters of this book into publication.

My dear friends – Tamar and Nir Brosh, and Noga and Jan Mueller – were there all along, lovingly accompanying the birth of each chapter and immersing themselves in the materials. For a while, we were all Camus and film-philosophy enthusiasts! Thank you for the patience, listening and fiery conversations.

Abbreviations

Works by Albert Camus

C   *Caligula and Other Plays*, 1984

MS   *The Myth of Sisyphus*, 2005

TR   *The Rebel*, 2013

TS   *The Stranger*, 1988

Camus' absurd and science fiction film: A potential point of convergence?

In this book, I will examine the relevance of Albert Camus' philosophy of the absurd to science fiction films – in particular, the subgenre involving encounters with nonhuman beings.[1] To establish such a connection, I will invoke aspects of the Camusean analysis of the absurd to explain and understand four films from this subgenre. I will then test whether the context offered by this type of film enables a new understanding of Camus' "feeling of the absurd" (Nagel 1971; Pölzler 2018) and the various tensions he considers inherent to human existence.

Yet, quite justifiably, various questions arise: Why science fiction films? And why Camus? What reason is there to connect the two? What leads me to believe that Camusean analysis of the absurd in the human condition could provide a fertile ground for a fresh perspective on science fiction film?

The philosophy of science fiction film

Over the last two decades, many philosophers have been increasingly inclined to consider film – and, more specifically, science fiction film – as a source of philosophical inquiry (Sanders 2008: 1; Litch 2010: 2). The

---

1 This is not an accepted classification in film studies. Based on the *Science Fiction Handbook* (Booker and Thomas 2009), it could be thought of as a synthesis of two subgenres: the alien invasion narrative and cyberpunk and posthuman science fiction. For the purposes of my analysis, this subgenre includes science fiction films involving an encounter with an apparently competitive, self-conscious "other": clones, artificial intelligence, androids, humanoids, aliens, and so forth.

more that is written on the subject, the clearer it is that opinions on the exact philosophical nature of film differ starkly. Scholars seem to share the view that films do not construct proper or explicit philosophical arguments in the way they approach fundamental questions (Anderson 2018; Baggini 2018). Some, however, consider film "an external embodiment" of philosophical thought (Rowlands 2005: 3), and, as such, an "effective tool for introducing a philosophical topic" (Litch 2010: 4). Others believe that films are more than mere tools for illustrating philosophical arguments and suggest that they may provoke philosophical thinking and both echo and develop philosophical ideas (Sanders 2008: 1). Finally, a more provocative approach, most prominently expressed by Stephen Mulhall (2016: 3–10), rejects both previous approaches on the basis that their use of film only serves to reconfirm theories to which they are already committed. Maintaining that films are, in fact, active participants in the making of philosophy, Mulhall argues for their capacity to expand philosophy beyond the reach of formal arguments.[2]

There is, however, agreement among many scholars that films can be "philosophical exercises" (Mulhall 2016: 4), an extended form of the philosophical thought-experiment. The traditional thought-experiment is conceived by the philosopher's imagination within the "laboratory of the mind"; it tests a hypothetical situation, which often transcends current technology or laws of nature, to "illustrate a puzzle, lay bare a contradiction in thought, and move us to provide further clarification" (Schneider 2016: 1). Similarly, films introduce us to a fictional world, often with "sufficient context" to interpret their key elements as a thought-experiment (Litch 2010: 5).

In his 1938 review of Jean-Paul Sartre's novel *Nausea*, Camus offers an explanation that could be indirectly applied to the discussion of film as philosophy: A "novel is never anything but a philosophy put into images" and, therefore, a good novel is one whose entire philosophy has been successfully translated into images (Camus, quoted in Golomb 2005: 120). Great novelists are philosophers who have preferred "writing in images"

2 Sorfa (2016: 3) supports this argument, suggesting that at least some films are capable of doing philosophy – "in a way that is unique to the medium," of course.

over "reasoned arguments," since they have had more confidence in the "educative message of perceptible appearance" (ibid.). They have insisted on relying solely on what experience allows them to say (Hughes 2007: 62).[3]

When we consider films as philosophical thought-experiments translated into perceptible appearances, science fiction seems to be a genre whose philosophical exercises are often centered on the nature of human consciousness and existence (Sanders 2008: 1). Knight and McKnight suggest that "it is a feature of this genre to pose such questions as, What is it to be human?" (Sanders 2008: 26–27). A continuation of the "early myths and epic sagas of many narrative traditions," science fiction employs the dimensions of space and time in order to gain perspective on our place in the universe; the cosmos is therefore a backdrop against which the interior space and present angst of the human are explored (Sardar 2002: 1).

While science fiction films seem to both pose fundamental questions and attempt to answer them in their own way through the perceptible realization of thought-experiments, in order to become a fully realized philosophy, they require philosophers. They "demand to be understood metaphysically" (Mulhall 2016: 7). They may evoke new philosophical thought-patterns, which should then be passed into philosophy to become illuminated for the viewer. After all, even Camus, who preferred concrete

---

3 Camus' 1956 novel, *The Fall*, is an interesting case in which Camus deviates from his own rule according to which a good novel should have its hidden philosophy wholly translated into images. While generally possessing characteristics of the conventional novel, Roberts (2008: 876) regards it as an "essay-novel," an uncategorizable hybrid "similar in form and content to a long and personalized philosophical essay in the manner of Kierkegaard or of Plato's dialogues." Its discourse explicitly covers a diverse philosophical territory, addressing ontological, ethical, political, and aesthetic topics, but without taking care to develop its ideas in a "tight sequential, logical fashion" (ibid., 882). This style, Roberts argues, aims to foster in the reader a reflection that cannot be achieved through abstract philosophical ideas, since *The Fall* uniquely considers these ideas "in relation to their contexts"; it thus allows us to recognise the imperfections, tensions and contradictions, as well as the power and insight of these ideas (ibid., 882). Roberts concludes that *The Fall* demonstrates Camus' ability to "bridge different genres of writing: to allow the literary to become philosophical via the forms of reflection engendered in the reader" (ibid., 885).

experience over thought, felt compelled to supplement his literary works by writing essays, as essays constitute the more abstract and argumentative form. Art, he stated, has the power to awaken many people to authentic life, but this awakening can only be completed through the elucidation of the implications of the art's philosophy (Golomb 2005: 120–121). Thus, to evaluate the contribution of this genre to philosophical discussion on human consciousness and existence, we must add "philosophy's voice" (Mulhall 2016: 10); that is, we must engage in a philosophical dialogue with the films.

One of the most intriguing ways in which this genre's thought-experiments explore the nature of human experience is through imagining encounters with nonhumans. Where does the urge to envisage self-aware artificial intelligences and beastly or godlike aliens come from? Schelde (1993: 3–4) argues that sci-fi nonhumans are merely a new manifestation of the monsters, ogres, trolls and elves of olden times. Such anthropomorphic folkloric creatures could thrive only so long as nature remained uncapturable and elusive; as soon as science tamed the wild by offering explanations of the natural world, forests once teeming with dwarfs and fairies became just forests. Since outer space, with its billions of galaxies, now represents the new unknown it has begun to accommodate space monsters and sprites

While this may account for the cultural and psychological dynamics that brought sci-fi nonhumans into being, their philosophical value remains undetermined. Rowlands (2005: 1–2) claims that this is the very "intellectual underpinning of sci-fi": The stark otherness serves as a mirror through which we see our own reflection; as we stare at the monster, we realize that it is ourselves who are staring back at us. In discussing the role of sci-fi aliens, Sardar (2002: 6) suggests that they are the "dark antithesis" that make the patches of light within the narrative's structure appear brighter, thereby throwing into sharp relief the nature of humanness. The aliens demonstrate that which is not human in order to illustrate that which is human; indeed, by reinforcing our sense of self, they complete the "chain of science fiction as normative genre" (ibid., 6). When Knight and McKnight analyze *Blade Runner* (Sanders 2008: 21–37), they deal not with what it is to be replicants, but with what it is to be human.

Philosophically, there can be no definition for something or someone that has no "other." A definition is possible only through comparison. Given that, in our present human condition, we do not have any self-reflective other who could hold up a mirror to us, this subgenre could represent one possible way for humans to transcend their anthropocentric worldview and outline the boundaries of human existence and consciousness. As the "conception of 'us' would lose meaning" in the absence of aliens, we need aliens to define a "conceptual, epistemological and innate" boundary (Sardar 2002: 9–10).[4] Moreover, their threatening non-humanity, and sometimes inhumanity, often lead us to re-evaluate human values and human instincts (ibid., 4).

This capacity to test the limits and limitations of human existence is, perhaps, the original contribution of science fiction film – and, more specifically, the subgenre involving nonhuman encounters – to philosophical thinking. By placing humans within larger cosmic contexts and in contact with unfamiliar elements, they delineate and clarify the frontiers of human nature. Whether it is an individual's journey in space, a malignant or benign alien invasion, or humanity's end of days, human beings are set against archetypal antitheses in order to call into question the preconceived metaphysical notions of viewers and to trouble the limits of their experience as "finite and embodied beings" (Anderson, 2018).

4 In this book I ignore the somewhat justified political criticism of many American science fiction films, which posits that what truly hides behind the mask of the alien "other" is the subaltern non-white or non-American other. For instance, American films of the postwar era should be suspected for having projected fear of the Japanese onto sci-fi epics in the form of "alien invasion" (S. Skrimshire 2018, personal communication, 17 July). I, however, limit myself to the metaphysical nonhuman/human interpretation.

Camus' philosophy of the absurd

The very phrase "Camus' philosophy" seems to pose a problem: Can Camus' absurdism be considered a real philosophy? This question has stirred up a great deal of controversy among philosophers – both in relation to Camus' stature as a philosopher, which he himself questioned,[5] and the philosophical wholeness of his notion of the absurd.

While highly esteemed for his literary genius, Camus' importance as a philosopher has been disparaged even by the "few scholars still interested" in him (Golomb 2005: 119). Golomb suggests that Camus is at least partially responsible for this, as he refuted his association with existentialism and was content to employ only "the explicatory-descriptive side of phenomenology," in contrast to Heidegger's and Sartre's efforts to ground their intuitions in valid systems (ibid., 119, 141). Foley (2008: 5) adds that nowadays the term "absurd" appears only rarely in academic discourse, including discussions dedicated to existentialist philosophy.

One of the most widespread criticisms of Camus' philosophical works is that they unequivocally fail the test of formal arguments. His ideas appear in the "fragmented fashion typical of artistic works" (Sagi 2002: 1). The unsystematic, perhaps even anti-systematic, nature of his philosophy has led most scholars to overlook its depth and complexity (Aronson 2017: 2). Some, on the other hand, compare Camus' philosophical endeavor with the work of Plato, Montaigne, Kierkegaard and Nietzsche, all of whom have made major contributions to philosophy, despite not being philosophers in the modern academic sense (Sagi 2002: 2; Golomb 2005: 119; Zaretsky 2013: 50–51). As I shall argue in Part I, the fact that Camus does not follow conventional pathways does not necessarily prevent him from constructing a relatively coherent universe, with its own metaphysics, ontology, epistemology, methodology, and ethics.

There is, however, a much deeper reason why Camus has remained an outsider to philosophy. As Zaretsky (2013: 13) points out, in *The Myth*

---

5 Zaretsky (2013: 48) describes how Camus, in a meeting with the British philosopher A. J. Ayer, "agreed with Ayer's dim view of his philosophical reasoning."

of Sisyphus Camus determinedly left behind philosophy's traditional terminology and methodology. One could even think of this central essay on
the absurd as a protest against philosophy's failure to respond to the "one
truly serious philosophical problem" (MS, 1). The essay is "a philosophy
that contests philosophy itself" (Aronson 2017: 2), one that rejects the very
idea of a philosophical system and, when confronted with the immediate
and pressing question of whether life is worth living at all, it occasionally
abandons the solid ground of argument and analysis altogether in favor
of metaphors and impressions. This led Francis Jeanson to claim that absurdist philosophy is a contradiction in terms, not a philosophy but "an
anti-rational posture that ends in silence" (ibid., 2); yet, such an exaggerated
contention fails, in my opinion, to capture the complexity and coherent
logic of Camus' ideas. After all, Camus never opposed rationality and
reason, but rather clarified their limited efficaciousness for comprehending
"the ever-resurgent irrational" (MS, 34).

In some respects, Camus' absurd has a philosophical status similar to
that of "film as philosophy." Both clearly carry philosophical content, but
their tendency to elude the explicit argument, prioritize experience and
convert thinking into impression and metaphor – thus creating Mulhall's
"philosophy in action" (2016: 4) – leads systematic idea-makers to regard
them with suspicion. They thrive on the "open border" between philosophy
and art (Baggini 2018).[6] This shared destiny may prove to be the cause of
important mutual influence.

Hughes (2007: 55) suggests that the "one truly philosophical problem,"
as presented by Camus, is located either "at the limits or even outside philosophy itself." Absurd reasoning requires the very act of philosophizing
to stretch beyond an unduly narrow conception of philosophy when confronted with this fundamental life-or-death question. If anything, the role
of philosophical thought is, in this case, to systematically negate itself by
acknowledging its limits. In his rejection of not only every existing answer
to the question, "What is the meaning of existence?" but also our very
capacity to answer, Camus shifts his concern to an experience that is of

---

6 A paraphrase of Mulhall's statement that he has "a sense that there is an open border
between philosophy and literature" (Baggini 2018).

"extremely limited philosophical import" (ibid., 56). Since this matter is simultaneously too humble and too emotional, it needs to be captured at the experiential level before it can be reached by philosophy (Aronson 2017: 6). Above all else, the absurd is a feeling, which arises arbitrarily, and it is therefore beyond argument and justification.[7] Put simply, it cannot be "philosophically justified" (Golomb 2005: 123).[8]

The concept of the absurd – the lucid recognition of human reality as a juxtaposition of "a yearning for the absolute" and an "awareness of the limitations and finality of human ability" (Sagi 1994: 283) – begins as a feeling and as an experience. It is therefore plausible to assume that, since the feeling of the absurd conveys more than any explanation of the absurd could, "it is up to other forms of discourse," the various arts in particular, to make up for the limitations of theoretical philosophy (Hughes 2007: 57). In Camus' words, "If the world were clear, art would not exist" (MS, 95).

The absurd unveils a truth about the human condition that eludes formal arguments (Zaretsky 2013: 45). It is perhaps for this reason that *The Stranger* preceded *The Myth*; only after we have come into contact with the feeling that permeates Meursault's life, as much as it permeates our own, can we advance to the essay – and even this evades justification and centers on a description and "diagnosis" of the human predicament (Golomb 2005: 120). The right order is from art to the "phenomenology of the 'notion of the absurd'" (ibid., 120–121). The absurd is a crisis of meaning, lurking at every corner, waiting to strike at any moment, evoking the painful "Why?" in the face of a silent and indifferent universe. Yet, Camus appears uninterested in destabilizing this inherent tension by answering the question; the unsettling feeling and its manifestations – weariness, anxiety, strangeness, nausea, and horror in the face of one's mortality – should be pursued all the way to their origin (Pölzler 2018: 2). Camus strives to maintain the

---

7 The Camusean notion of the feeling of the absurd as a primordial condition that lays the foundations for the concept of the absurd (MS, 27) can be compared with Ratcliffe's definition of "existential feelings", that is, feelings that relate to "the world as a whole", rather than intentional states, which are directed at objects in the world (2012: 1–2).

8 Though, as I will argue in Chapter 2, the essential origin of the feeling can be detected and analyzed.

sense of a "consciousness astonished at itself at the core of human existence" (Zaretsky 2013: 13).

Even some of Camus' critics, among them analytic philosophers, have acknowledged the unfailing presence of the absurd in human life. Ayer recognizes an undeniable "emotional significance" in *The Myth* (ibid., 47). Nagel (1971: 718) believes that although the arguments for absurdity are logically feeble, they seem to "express something that is difficult to state, but fundamentally correct." He regards this absurd predicament as a feature of our very humanness (ibid., 726). The absurd, as a pre-philosophical, concrete reality, may be more conceivable. It is "an experience to be lived through" (TR, 8).

All of this raises the possibility that, in the same way that Camus felt compelled to move back and forth, from literary and theatrical expression to essays and vice versa, a different, less philosophically rigid medium is required to help us to bring the experience of the absurd and Camus' vision of the human–cosmos relationship more sharply into view – a medium that is ideally located on the border that loosely separates philosophy from art.

The choice to employ science fiction film for this task has at least three advantages: First, film strives to create symbolic and imaginative representations of the world that remain believable and consonant with our actual human experience to enable us to reveal something we have not noticed before or to "make sense of it in a different and helpful way" (Baggini, 2018).[9] Second, the perceptible thought-experiments of science fiction film are largely centered on asking, and attempting to answer, life's most urgent questions regarding the nature and meaning of the human phenomenon. A third advantage, however, may best explain the suitability of science fiction film; I shall elaborate on this third advantage in the following section.

---

9 Baggini (2018) goes further by claiming that this is where film and philosophy may overlap: their aspiration to "represent reality to us truthfully in such a way as to make us understand it better or more accurately than before," with the exception that film shows rather than says.

The thematic and methodological interconnection of absurdism and science fiction film

Camus' philosophy of the absurd is almost completely absent from discussions of the philosophy of film, and the philosophy of science fiction film in particular.[10] This is intriguing, since there is a strong thematic and methodological link between the two: They are both engaged in testing and exploring the limits of human experience through humankind's relationship with the cosmos, either in the form of another species or with the universe as the ultimate other. Furthermore, both are doing this – Camus consciously and the films through a suggestive philosophical interpretation – in the hope of extricating not only the nature of humanness, but also the human potential to attain lucidity, authenticity, freedom and even happiness.

If Schelde's (1993: 3–4) assertion that science fiction film weaves our modern mythology is right, Camus' own myth – that of Sisyphus as the archetypal human – fits into this mythology well. At the core of the Sisyphean experience, there is an unresolvable tension between human consciousness and the cosmos. Camus painstakingly describes this inherent tension as the friction between longing and limit: the longing for meaning and the inability to find it; the longing for reason and lucidity and the limit of knowing; the longing for unity and the limit of separation; the longing for rebellion and the limit of a predetermined fate; the longing for tomorrow and the limit of death, and the longing for the heights and the limits of circularity and repetitiveness. The foundation of all of these frictions is a consciousness struggling with the recognition of its barriers and finitude: "lucid reason noting its limits" (MS, 47).

This is perfectly congruent with science fiction's – and especially the nonhuman subgenre's – philosophical inclination toward marking or questioning the boundaries of human existence. Just as science fiction makes

---

10 One exception is Alan Woodfolk, who explores Camus' absurdism in film noir (Conard 2006: 107–124), as well as in the science fiction film *Alphaville* (Sanders 2008: 191–205).

use, as a part of its methodology, of either posthuman beings or aliens to gain perspective on the nature of human existence within the empty cosmic vastness, so the absurd negatively emphasizes and reinforces the walls that surround man, only to draw strength from these walls (MS, 58). The enclosing walls are the source of the absurdist enlightenment.

A long list of science fiction films weave their philosophical tension around the human longing to know and to unite and the limit of the cosmic silence.[11] It seems that such films send humans off on dumbfounding journeys through outer space to test the friction between alienation and unity. Humans are often left hovering in an infinitely vacant universe, forced to come to terms with their insatiable longing. The astonishing beauty of the cosmic landscape is at once "inhuman" and "remote."[12] Ironically, the broadened context aggravates the sense of limitation, the fundamental experience Buber (2004: 157) described as being "homeless in infinity." The scale of the unfolding cosmos intensifies human smallness and, with it, the absurdist pathos.

It is important to recognize that science fiction film is the folklore of an era and also, for the most part, a mythology narrated by one specific civilization. It usurps whatever point in space it reaches and lands on in order to establish "Western epistemology and metaphysics" (Sardar 2002: 12).[13] Its imagined futures carry with them the complexes of the modern mind, including the psychological complexes evoked by its science and technology. Sagi (2002: 12) asserts that the experience of the absurd, as captured by Camus, is a "symptom of modern life" rather than an inherent attribute of human existence – indeed, it is the outcome of the Copernican revolution, which robbed humans of the feeling that the universe could be their home. Hemmed in by the unlimited on every side, humans were forced

---

11 See, for example, *2001: A Space Odyssey* 1968; *The Abyss* 1989; *Contact* 1997; *Dark City* 1998; *Prometheus* 2012; *Interstellar* 2014; *Moon* 2009; *Gravity* 2013.

12 Here I borrow words Camus used to describe the absurdist characteristic of man's encounter with nature (MS, 12–13).

13 Sci-fi films are also produced in Russia and Asia, for instance, yet they are often treated as "American" and "Western" products or as imitations; moreover, one cannot deny the clear hegemonic position of Hollywood in science fiction film production (Fritzsche 2014: 3).

into the discovery that they were different from the rest of creation. Thus, the absurd came into being – or, at least, intensified – with the emergence of the highly subjective, individual self-consciousness (ibid., 8). Later scientific breakthroughs, which on the surface seemed to get us closer to the mystery of the universe – such as the growing cosmological awareness of its immeasurable magnitude – have only further illustrated the randomness of the appearance of an isolated and bewildered self-reflective awareness on one floating planet in the midst of expanses without horizons.

It is for this reason that visions of the future in science fiction film are accompanied by a sense of disconcerting estrangement. The highly advanced yet cold-hearted technology, gloomy spaceships gliding into the coolness of cosmic space, unfathomable black holes, and the strange appearances of the "others" all serve as effective magnifiers of the experience of the absurd. Wherever humans travel, be it "down here" or "out there," the absurd awaits them patiently, ready to toss them back onto themselves. As I will suggest later, it may be more accurate to state that we take our alienation with us: an embodied self-awareness that hits against the walls of its longing in whatever corner of the universe it finds itself in.[14]

It is therefore reasonable to seek new layers of insight into the experience of the absurd by utilizing a filmic genre that has constructed the ideal setting for it: The tangible limits that are created by placing humans in relation to extra-human elements force men and women to turn their gaze to the mirror of the absurd and to consciously choose concrete ways of facing this inescapable fate. The reality of the absurd, which in daily life may only be fleetingly experienced, pressing in on one gently, becomes acute and undeniable in light of such sharp contrasts. But before we delve into examples of the subgenre of nonhumans, we must first gain a deeper understanding of the concept and the experience of limits and the many different expressions of limits in Camus' philosophy.

The book's first part – "Camus' absurd: Consciousness and limits" – aims to introduce the main components of Camus' absurdity in such a

---

14 This, we will see, is most ironically noticeable in films that deal with artificial intelligences that assimilate human emotions and behaviors (for instance, *2001: A Space Odyssey* 1968; *Blade Runner* 1982; *A.I. Artificial Intelligence* 2001; *Never Let Me Go* 2010; *Cloud Atlas* 2012; *Her* 2013; *Ex-Machina* 2014).

way that it can be easily applied to the analysis of the films later. Since Camus himself ascribed to the novel, and to art in general, greater capacities to capture the "feeling of the absurd," I ground my elucidation of absurdity in my analysis of *The Stranger* and *Caligula*, thus establishing the arts, and consequently film, as a more immediate way of approaching the absurdity of the human condition. In Chapter 1, I demonstrate the way *The Stranger* silently and metaphorically thrusts us into the territory of the absurd, revealing that the principle that limits not only define human nature, but also hold a surprising redemptive power is at the heart of the absurd. Chapter 2 explores the concept of the absurd, more coherently presented in *The Myth of Sisyphus*, as a collision between human consciousness and five untraversable limits – separation, knowing, meaning, death, and repetition. I argue that the source of absurdity is the very existence of a self-transcendent, observing consciousness, and that since it is consciousness itself that produces absurdity, it will take absurdity with it to any imaginable universe or future. In Chapter 3, drawing on *The Myth* and *The Rebel*, I turn to the consequences of awakening to the feeling of absurdity and the ways in which one could or should live in the light of this feeling. I consider the variety of possible responses proposed by Camus to this recognition of the absurdity of the human condition: from the five negative responses of suicide, murder, nihilism, hope, and renunciation, to the five positive responses of acceptance, revolt, freedom, passion, and human solidarity.

Equipped with these Camusean essentials, I delve, in the second part – "Science fiction films: Absurd at the edge of the cosmos" – into an in-depth analysis of four science fiction films (the rationale for the selection of these four films will be addressed in the concluding chapter). Chapter 4 analyzes, side by side, two first-contact films – Robert Zemeckis' *Contact* (1997) and Denis Villeneuve's *Arrival* (2016) – to test the validity of Camus' metaphysics in a universe where human estrangement seems to be disrupted by cosmic visitors. Similarly, Chapter 5 analyzes, side by side, Steven Spielberg's *A.I. Artificial Intelligence* (2001) and Spike Jonze's *Her* (2013). Whereas the sudden descent of *Contact*'s and *Arrival*'s aliens is experienced as the appearance of the ultimate other who mirrors our relationship with a silent universe, it is the disturbing closeness of these A.I. forms to the human experience that starkly reflects the absurd tensions of the human experience and potential responses to these. Lastly, in Chapter 6, I bring together the conclusions of all four films to derive from them more general insights in the light of Camus' absurdity. I confirm the argument put forward in Part I that absurdity is, first and foremost, a collision within ourselves, and therefore, a friction that should also be expected to afflict us at the edge of the universe, in a far-off future. Furthermore, I show that these analyses yield more than an insightful reflection of the absurd in science fiction film. Indeed, imaginative collisions with nonhumans seem to tell us a lot about the nature of the absurd in the human condition, as well as raising the question of whether absurdity is exclusively a human matter. Ultimately, my interpretation of the films illuminates the films themselves just as much as it illuminates, challenges, and expands Camus' concept of absurdity, thus contributing to our current understanding of what the absurd reality is and how we can either live with it or transcend it.

PART I

Camus' absurd: Consciousness and limits

CHAPTER I

The redemptive power of absurd walls in *The Stranger*

As far as we can tell, Camus' commitment to the absurd as a literary and philosophical mission began in May 1936, the same month he defended his dissertation on the subject of Christian metaphysics and Neoplatonism at the University of Algiers (Zaretsky 2013: 14). "Philosophical work: Absurdity," he wrote in his journal.[1] Two years later, he reiterated the sentiment two more times in his journal. While he was still in the research and contemplation phase, he determined to tackle the subject, almost simultaneously, in three different genres: a novel, a play, and an essay. *Caligula* came first;[2] *The Stranger*, the "novel of the absurd,"[3] followed, and, shortly thereafter, *The Myth of Sisyphus*, the "essay on the absurd," came into being (ibid., 15–16).

---

1 Why this subject sparked in him interest in absurdism is a matter of speculation. No doubt, his awareness of it was ignited by his supervisor, the French philosopher Jean Grenier, who encouraged him to read existentialists such as Kierkegaard, Chestov, and Berdyaev (Srigley 2007: 4). We also know that apart from his teachers, the one who stirred Camus' thought the most was Nieztsche: his name repeatedly appears in Camus' early *Notebooks* and Nietzsche's *Birth of Tragedy* is often referenced in his Master's thesis (ibid., 5). McBride (1992) devoted his study to demonstrating the influence of Saint Augustine and Nietzcshe as well as Camus' dissertation as a whole on his later development of absurdist notions. His principal argument is that Camus' absurdism derived from his ambiguous relationship with Christianity and from his unfulfilled longing for unity with God. And Walker argues that the Plotinian conception of one's desire for a homeland and the existential unease due to its loss, or absence, re-emerged in its absurdist form in *The Myth of Sisyphus* (Srigley 2007: 16).

2 In terms of the realization of the three projects, *Caligula* came last: It was first performed in 1945.

3 I have borrowed the term from Bombert's 1948 article title "Camus and the Novel of the 'Absurd.'"

Naming this creative cycle the "three absurds" (Sharpe 2015: 41), Camus' initial intention was to have the works published as a single volume (Foley 2008: 14). Although the three belonged to different genres, he clearly conceived of them as a unified, profoundly interconnected body of work. When all three of the works had been completed, he declared, "Beginnings of liberty," as if he had to get the absurd off his chest (Sharpe 2015: 41). The Myth of Sisyphus was only his first "myth," one of a prospective trio that he never managed to complete,[4] yet although he "progressed beyond" his three absurds, he "remained faithful" to the "exigency which prompted them" (Camus 1955: vi).

Among the various critiques *The Stranger* was met with upon its release in 1942 – all of which were rejected by Camus, regardless of whether they were good or mixed, as "based on misunderstandings" (Zaretsky 2013: 43) – Sartre's "Explication of *The Stranger*" stood out for its undeniable lucidity. Sartre, Zaretsky writes, filtered the baffling novel "through the insights of the philosophical essay" (ibid., 43). Obviously inspired by Camus' own distinction between the "feeling of the absurd" and the "notion of the absurd" (MS, 27), Sartre argued that *The Myth* aims at "giving us this idea" whereas *The Stranger* is intended to give us the feeling. Indeed, just as the feeling of the absurd "lays the foundations" for the concept but is not limited to it and can even go further thanks to its aliveness (MS, 27), so *The Stranger* silently thrusts us into the territory of the absurd, leaving it to *The Myth* to "illumine the landscape" (Golomb 2005: 141).[5]

---

4 Sisyphus was meant to be followed by the myth of Prometheus and the myth of Nemesis. An even broader plan consisted of five stages: absurd, revolt, judgment, love, and "creation corrected," each expressed in the form of a novel, a play, and an essay (Sharpe 2015: 41). Roberts (2008: 875–876) notes that Camus' 1956 novel, *The Fall*, was his only deviation from these carefully-planned cycles: though in some respects it is a complement to *The Stranger*, it "came into being more by accident."

5 Here I mention once again a suggestion I made in the introduction: such a relationship between feeling and concept could easily be applied to film and Camus' philosophy of the absurd. Films, probably even more than novels, engage not only our intellectual, but also our imaginative and emotional faculties in ways that engender a phenomenological and visceral, as well as a more straightforwardly conceptual, grasp of the issue, hence their superior capacity to capture and explore this almost pre-reflexive absurd feeling.

Brombert (1948: 119) justifiably questions Sartre's consideration of the essay as a key to the novel. Claiming that such an approach is "neither logical nor truly critical," Brombert comments that the reader of *The Stranger* cannot be expected to have read *The Myth*. While a writer's essays may be used to further elucidate his or her works, they cannot be treated as a starting point: A literary work should contain its own explanation, functioning as both the "communicating vehicle" and that which is communicated (ibid., 121). On the basis of this rationale, I would like to suggest going in the other direction, that is, I would like to consider *The Stranger* not as a representation of the absurd hero that merely "exhibits"[6] and never really lives, but rather as a starting point that can shed more light on the concept of the absurd as presented in *The Myth* and even go further. From this perspective, *The Myth* branches out from *The Stranger* as its "philosophical twin," transforming images into thoughts (Golomb 2005: 130). I choose to take this approach not to protect *The Stranger*'s literary independence, but because I believe that it is more faithful to Camus' own intention, as well as the nature of Camus' absurdism. As such, it can generate the most insightful reading of the two texts.

In the introduction I contended that as far as Camus' absurdism is concerned, the right order is from art to the "phenomenology of the 'notion of the absurd'" (Golomb 2005: 120–121). This cannot be otherwise, because in a universe devoid of abstract realities and Platonic essences, the "concrete signifies nothing more than itself" (MS, 94) and therefore all thought can do is cover "with images what has no reason" (ibid., 95). Nowadays philosophy serves appearances and not the other way around: While universal concepts bend before life's particularities and pluralities, reason cannot "comprehensively explain," but it can "lucidly describe" (Sharpe 2015: 43–45), as well as imitate, life and duplicate its experiences (MS, 92). Camus' 1952 praise of Melville's writings reflects his own approach of absurd creation: "In Melville the symbol grows out of reality, the image springs from perception" (Dunwoodie 2007: 162).

---

6 See, for example, Foley's interpretation (2008: 14–22), which starts with Sisyphus and, from there, delves into the novel as a demonstration of the essay's concepts of "wild courage and rebellious scorn."

As well as recognizing that in an absurd universe a philosophical novel communicates more of the feeling and experience of the absurd than an essay does, Camus believes that fiction is better able to combat the immanent nihilism of such a universe.[7] To promote the "ideal of authentic life," which transcends "rational discourse," one requires concrete images rather than abstracts – emotionally engaging images that effectively arouse sufficient pathos and "existential anguish," which enable readers to transcend nihilism and grow in authenticity (Golomb 2005: 120). The philosophical novel frees the universe from illusion and populates it instead with "truths of flesh and blood" to entice the reader to revolt without hope (MS, 99).

By first grounding ourselves in the novel, considering it a more capable vehicle for the feeling and experience of the absurd – and accordingly reading *The Myth* as its conceptual extension and transformation into thought – we may arrive at an interpretation that differs from those offered by most commentators. *The Stranger* has engendered a great deal of social, cultural, political, and psychological readings.[8] Indeed, it was Camus himself who insisted that the novel possessed a "social" meaning too (Foley 2008: 21), explicitly encouraging the reader to focus on the main character's refusal to "play the game" and subject himself to collective untruthfulness (Ohayon 1983: 189). Yet even a commentator such as Foley (2008: 21), who follows Camus' advice, recognizes that the social intention is suffocated by the "sheer metaphysical weight" of the novel's wish to convey the inner and intimate journey of the absurd mind.[9]

This reading reveals the novel to be the description of the step-by-step process of the awakening of a dormant consciousness to the reality of

---

7 See, for instance, Camus' claim in his preface to Nicolas Chamfort works: "[O]ur greatest moralists are not makers of maxims – they are novelists" (quoted in Sharpe 2015: 45–46).

8 See, for example, the psychological analyses of Stamm 1969; Slochower 1969, Ohayon 1983, and Scherr 2014. See also O'Brien's overtly political reading from 1970; Dunwoodie's cultural interpretation from 2007, and philosophical readings, such as Golomb 2005 and Foley 2008, which place the novel within the context of individual/society relations, as the absurd individual's struggle for integrity.

9 This is Brombert's central criticism (1948: 121–123): the novel's literary weakness is that Camus breathes into the main character's nostrils the "life of his own mind," forcing him to express the author's ideas.

the absurd: its initial failure to respond to it; the methodical approach it employs in order to embrace it, and the inner liberation it consequently achieves. As Zaretsky (2013: 45–46) puts it, *The Stranger* is, above all, a portrayal of a man "forming a mind": the emergence of a genuine self-reflection. Thus, deciphering the novel's symbols extricates and sheds light on the very same methodology applied by Camus in *The Myth*, with its first part corresponding to the first 26 pages of *The Myth* (capturing, conceptually rather than phenomenologically, the feeling of the absurd), its second part to pages 27–114 (the persistent negation of all hope), and its ending to pages 115–119 (the absurd elevation). I contend that at the heart of *The Stranger* lies the same principle that guides the journey of *The Myth* – that limits, whether they are *The Stranger*'s concrete prison walls or *The Myth*'s abstract absurd walls, not only define human nature, but also hold a surprising redemptive power, which is the crux of the absurdist enlightenment.

Part I: An initial awakening

Much of *The Stranger*'s first part is narrated in a literary style that directly expresses the climate of the absurd. As Sartre observed, its "atomistic sentences in the present tense," of "arbitrary facticity" and with no rational connection to bind them, isolate each moment from all others, emptying life of any "meaningful context" (Golomb 2005: 131–132). Devoid of past or future, Meursault slides through "an endless procession of present moments" (Zaretsky 2013: 23), embodying what *The Myth* later captured as "that series of unrelated actions which becomes his fate" (MS, 119).

Yet this style, which describes but never explains, establishes more than the feeling of the absurd: The broken reality reflects a disjointed consciousness, which does not yet exist as a self-reflective mind.[10] The hollow narrative nearly caricatures Hume's "bundle" theory of the self;

---

10 For the most part, I will use in this chapter, and in Part I as a whole, the term "consciousness" in a way that does not deviate from Husserl's and Sartre's conception of it;

its use of language allows us to penetrate into Meursault's "innermost life" only to realize that there is nothing there (Golomb 2005: 131–132). Not only is Meursault devoid of any interiority; he is literally incapable of self-awareness. When he glances at the mirror, all that is reflected in it is "a corner of my table with my alcohol lamp next to some pieces of bread" (TS, 24); there is simply "not yet a self to be seen" (Zaretsky 2013: 25). It is a "truly transparent" consciousness (Brombert 1948: 120), which requires other people and objects to mirror its own moods, like self-judgment, the need to cry, apathy and the inner voice that troubles it (TS, 10–11). As Golomb (2005: 130) states, the Meursault of the first part is far from a paragon of authenticity: His inability to lie reflects not courage, but rather a purely "spontaneous" and "uncomplicated" mind, which lacks any duality or struggle within itself (Dunwoodie 2007: 157).

This barely existent consciousness, nevertheless, is pushed to awaken by two elements: death and the light of truth. Death, the most unrejectable limit of consciousness and life, opens and concludes *The Stranger*. The confrontation with life's ultimate limit unconsciously ignites in Meursault the "Why?," the protest against meaninglessness. For the first time, consciousness opens one eye to regard reality, but it manages to fall asleep again (TS, 4, 7). That is because the death of another – even the death of a dear one – is not necessarily enough to shake one up completely. As Scherr (2014: 170, 176) suggests, in his Freudian reading of the novel, it may be that in the unconscious none of us believes in our own death, since we are unable to conceive of the death of our ego; only a fully conscious awareness of the frontiers of *our* life (as direct as Meursault's confrontation with death in the second part of *The Stranger*) has the potential to do that. This is echoed in *The Myth* when Camus argues that the death of others is but an unconvincing rumor and that there is no way to prepare for death, since all we know is life and consciousness (MS, 14).

Yet, as soon as death pierces Meursault's sleepy mind and life, light begins to agitate him. In front of his mother's closed casket, he is "blinded" by the light and the brightness of the room, and only feels more drowsy

---

that is, that consciousness is always consciousness of something (Sartre 2003: 650). However, on occasion, I use the term as, simply, the equivalent of "mind."

(TS, 8, 9); likewise, in *The Myth*, physical light turns into the subdued, abstract light of absurdity (MS, 9), which everyone evades, hoping for a "flight from light," as light provokes a painful lucidity "in the face of experience" (ibid., 3). Light, the second catalyst of awakening, is non-causal and random; it may strike "at any street corner" (ibid., 9), and its most demanding manifestation is the sun.

The sun in *The Stranger* is the sun of the absurd,[11] which has glowed ever since humanity committed the crime of patricide against the heavenly father. It is perhaps not coincidental that Nietzsche – "the most famous of God's assassins," according to Camus (MS, 106) – uses the same symbol when exclaiming that, with the murder of God, we have "unchained this earth from its sun" and are therefore "moving away from all suns" (Hollingdale 1999: 139). Meursault's consciousness is forced to awaken in light of the absurdist reality that radiates unbearably and scorchingly over his head, in a Nietzschean, godless, and amoral world. The sun is the uninvited "awareness of the immanent nature of the world," which rises as soon as the ethic that was our beacon has lost its power over us (Golomb 2005: 132).

As the bright light of the phenomenal world, the sun, when it shines moderately, illumines life's objects of pleasure and the sensual earth – like Camus' life-affirming sun in the *Noces* (Dunwoodie 2007: 152–154). When it grows in strength and becomes achingly dazzling, however, it lays bare the reality of the earth's emptiness and oppressive inhumanity (TS, 15) and compels the consciousness to actually see the "Nada that could only have originated in a country crushed by the sun" (Dunwoodie 2007: 155–156). In this intense state, the sun is undefeatable and all-pervasive: "If you go slowly, you risk getting sunstroke. But if you go too fast, you work up a sweat and then catch a chill inside the church" (TS, 17). There is no way

---

11 Ohayon (1983: 190–198) devotes his entire article to the contrary argument that *The Stranger*'s sun is the metaphor of "patriarchal absolutism" (ibid., 193), acting as the negative image of the father-God. Accordingly, Meursault is the rebellious son. This is disputable: first, the father-God is sufficiently represented in the novel by the magistrate and the chaplain, and second, it does not make sense that God, who is represented by moralists such as the magistrate and the chaplain, would urge Meursault to kill the Arab.

out: Wherever one goes, whether in the atheistic direction or the theistic direction, one would be confronted by the "inevitability of death," which renders one's life "absurd and unfulfilled" (Scherr 2014: 179).

Indeed, the awakened mind, which had formerly been protected by unselfconsciousness and apathy, might not find a way out, but it would at least seek relief in an absurd rebellion. Here, the paths of Meursault and Camus' other major absurd hero, Caligula, momentarily converge. Both characters conclude erroneously – Caligula in a far more deliberate tone – that an unbridled and destructive nihilistic outburst would be the proper response to the sun that blinds them. Both leave the funerals of loved ones with an "alarmed new consciousness of human mortality" (Scherr 2014: 186) and find themselves disorientedly driven to murder as a protest against death. Incapable of embracing it, it is as if they attempt to "murder" death itself,[12] and thereby initiate a seemingly predetermined chain of events that will inevitably lead to their deaths; in a way, they substitute suicide for murder.

Like Dostoevsky's Kirilov, who postulated that killing God means becoming a god yourself, but was unable to handle the freedom he granted himself (MS, 104–105), Meursault and Caligula infer that now "everything is unconditionally permitted," and assume the role of gods on earth by amorally "determining the fate of others" (Golomb 2005: 133–134). They think that they go all the way with the illogical logic of the absurd, yet the novel and the play alike demonstrate that such a rebellion does not have a liberating effect; what it does lead to is the disillusionment of realizing that this is the wrong type of freedom (C, 63). While one might be tempted to blame the sun, the sun does not in itself necessarily push one to nihilism; its role is only to show and to stimulate realization.

On the fateful day on which Meursault enacts the wrong type of freedom, two other symbols – which later become established in *The Myth* as concepts – are at play. The first is the sea, also represented by Meursault's lover Marie,[13] which momentarily enables the fulfillment of the longing for

---

12 This may be the cause of Meursault's unexplainable need to fire four more times at the Arab's clearly dead body (TS, 59).

13 According to Ohayon (1983: 202): "Marie, mare, mère, mer, sea." This may also echo the title for the Virgin Mary, "Our lady, Star of the Sea," in ancient traditions (S. Skrimshire 2019, personal communication, 8 January).

unity: "We felt a closeness as we moved in unison and were happy" (TS, 50). But since, in an absurd universe, one could never fully achieve unity with oneself, others, and the world as a whole, Meursault must be torn away from the experience to lucidly confront his reality – in the same way that Sisyphus, who enjoyed the smiling earth and the "sparkling sea" too much, would be snatched "from his joys" by the gods and dragged to his rock (MS, 116). Accordingly, the sea grows weaker and is finally replaced by the sun's "sea of molten lead" (TS, 57–58). The sun, which inflicts the same inescapable pain as on the day of the funeral, soon introduces the second symbol which completes it: silence (TS, 55). In this climate, where there is nothing besides awareness and emptiness, and everything closes in around him, Meursault vainly attempts to overpower and break the silence of the indifferent universe (TS, 59). Although the setting seems to evoke hopeless action, it is Meursault who finally disrupts the unity and happiness and chooses to place himself in the persistent tension between the longing for harmony and the impossibility of ever resting in its fulfillment.

Part II: Prison as home

The Stranger's second part is characterized by a distinct shift of consciousness, which is made immediately perceptible by its significantly more complex and sophisticated literary style. A language of "assessment and reason," "cogitation and memory," takes the place of the raw and immediate language of "physicality, need and desire" (Dunwoodie 2007: 157–159). This shift heralds Meursault's gradual evolution from an unthinking, transparent mind to a "self-reflexive consciousness" (ibid., 159–160). We are plunged into a rich subjective world of contradictory "feelings, motives and world outlook" (Golomb 2005: 131–132). Yet we are somewhat prepared, since Meursault's declaration at the end of Part I that he had shattered the "exceptional silence of a beach where I'd been happy" (TS, 59) gives away a newfound awareness of an internal mood.

But why does Meursault grow in "self-awareness once he is imprisoned" (Zaretsky 2013: 45)?[14] Slochower (1969: 294) and Ohayon (1983: 198–200) argue that shooting the Arab causes Meursault's consciousness to come alive and to consolidate a self. This "original sin," writes Ohayon, "cracked Sisyphus' rock" and extricated fossilized thoughts and feelings, thus activating an "intrapsychic life." However, this does not accord with Camus' line of thought, especially in the form it takes in *Caligula*. Both the play and the novel are pronounced statements against nihilism, and their acts of murder represent the mind's failed attempt to overcome absurd reality. If anything, it is Meursault's sobering up, his realization that that freedom was not the right one, that guided him toward a more mature way of handling the absurd – a way that ultimately enabled the crystallization of an authentic and reflective selfhood in him.[15] Rather than shattering the limits imposed on human consciousness, residing wholeheartedly within these confines allows one's existence to find its noblest fulfillment. Indeed, in a godless world, what awakens and delivers the individual is not the apparent freedom achieved by God's absence, but the intense limits one voluntarily forces upon oneself.[16]

With the disappearance of hope – represented by the cessation of Marie's visits – Meursault can finally feel "at home" in his cell (TS, 72). He is content to gaze at the sea through the small window, and to grip the bars with his face "straining toward the light," and he favors his quiet and dark cell over the dizzying visiting room with its "harsh light pouring out of the sky" (ibid., 73) – again rejecting the fulfillment of his longing for unity, while keeping this longing aflame. He renounces fantasies of freedom and accepts the identity of a prisoner, likening himself to one who lives

---

14 "Self-awareness," in this case, is literal: whereas in the first part, as previously noted, Meursault was unable to detect himself when looking at his mirror (TS, 24), now he gazes at his reflection and hears the sound of his own voice (ibid., 81).

15 Meursault, in this sense, is permitted by Camus to move beyond the point at which Caligula is halted.

16 One should note that the introspective style is significantly more prevalent from the second half of Part II onwards – further evidence that the realization of limits unifies Meursault's mind.

in the "trunk of a dead tree," from which he can only "look up at the sky" (ibid., 76–77).

There are good reasons to suspect that Meursault unconsciously drives himself into his cell and eventual death sentence, which implies that in order to achieve authenticity, one's consciousness directs itself toward the recognition of its limits. It is plausible that after his mother's death, Meursault felt compelled to demonstrate that indeed "there was no way out" (TS, 17) by simulating a seemingly deterministic act. Scherr (2014: 179–180) suggests that the Arab was Meursault's "surrogate for his own death," a way of intimately experiencing death "without dying himself." Ohayon (1983: 190–201) sides with this view from a different angle, pointing out that Meursault does not repent since he wants to be sentenced to death.[17] Grounding himself in Camus' own words, that Meursault is the "only Christ we deserved," Ohayon outlines the ways in which Meursault imitates Jesus' refusal to escape his fate by remaining silent, as well as Jesus' self-image as a sacrificial offering to the world (ibid., 190–201). Yet, just like Caligula, Meursault's wish for death cannot take the form of suicide, since the opposite of suicide is the "man condemned to death" (MS, 53) – and being condemned to death is the reality that the absurd hero must authentically confront.

While the sun was the great awakener of the first part, Part II introduces the reader to the second catalyst of lucidity: the confinement of the prison cell – the difference being that the sun is an aggressive cosmic intervention, whereas the cell is a conscious choice of the absurd hero. Such a hero determines to "make his rock, or his prison walls, everything that he has" (Skrimshire 2006: 296), since by realizing that this prison cell is "all we have and all we need," we gain a key to self-transformation (ibid., 297). Truly, we all await our death sentence in the cosmic cell, and all that we have left is the infinite sky above our head, which represents our eternal longing. And so, the only thing a human being should be interested in is execution (TS, 110) – an unwavering acknowledgment of the limit of our life and consciousness. Such an acute recognition of being hanged sooner

---

17 See also Clark (2017: 115), who demonstrates the different ways in which Meursault "could have claimed self-defense."

or later is one of the "few things" that "concentrate the mind" and cause an individual to come to oneself (Zaretsky 2013: 45–46). Indeed, the philosophical perspective conveyed through *The Stranger* seems to propose that one's authenticity is put to the test by the Heideggerian "Being-towards-death" and is formed by the manner in which one faces this terminal limit (Golomb 2005: 130).

Between these four absurd walls, Meursault – "the most faithful incarnation of Camus' absurd reasoning" (Skrimshire 2006: 288) – throws himself into an unsparing process of renunciation, which clarifies much of *The Myth*'s methodology of "persistence." Camus' philosophical criticism of scientific knowledge, religious belief and existentialist flight has one real purpose: to force the mind into a state of complete negation in order to allow an encounter with reality as it is. The "refusal to lie" is broadened to include even the subtlest form of mental escape. This is done with an "austere dignity" (Foley 2008: 22), a monk-like abstinence, which demonstrates that pushing the absurd to its "logical conclusions" (C, 45) does not imply a nihilistic freedom, but rather a radical form of self-constraint.

This brings to mind Camus' imagining of another absurd hero, Don Juan, sitting in a cell in a monastery, close to death and contemplating, "through a narrow slit in the sun-baked wall," a bland land in which he "recognizes himself" (MS, 74). Meursault, too, looks at the walls' stones for months, and finds in them neither metaphysical consolation nor earthly satisfaction (TS, 119). One by one, he abandons any comforting habits of the mind and body: desires and sensual passions, sex and smoking (ibid., 82), the knowledge of books (ibid., 108), and logical arguments (ibid., 114). When the priest enters, the last embodiment of hope, Meursault feels that his cell is crowded and uncomfortable (Scherr 2014: 173). He learns the absurd through his attempts to evade it (MS, 110), thus rejecting faith as a "safeguard against suffering and despair" (Henke 2017: 137) and removing the "little painted screens" that the priest holds in front of his face to "hide the scaffold" from him (MS, 88). That is not to say that he does not experience moments of tragic consciousness and revolt against the limits of existence during his own dark, endless night of Gethsemane, awaiting his Antichrist crucifixion (ibid., 118), yet the struggle to escape the absurd, he knows, is an inseparable part of the absurd.

An unexpected union

The Stranger's last pages (115–123) elucidate, by means of an emotionally captivating experience, the shift from persistent negation to the happy Sisyphus at the end of *The Myth*. They begin with Meursault's second violent outburst, this time at the prison chaplain. As the violent eruption at the end of Part I purged his being of nihilism and catalyzed a more mature response to the absurd, so the outburst near the end of Part II finally purifies his being of all hope, completes the process of negation and drives him toward absurd enlightenment. Herein lies the transforming potential of absurd revolt: Though it can never transcend the boundaries of absurdist reality, it ironically gives rise to the inner power needed to fully accept it.[18] This joyous blind rage washes Meursault clean (TS, 122), preparing him for the final outcome of absurd negation. Like the Arab, the chaplain is merely a reflection of an inner mode, in this case the remaining contradiction still buried within Meursault. By proving that he is able to disrupt the chaplain's complacency and metaphysical certainty (Henke 2017: 137), Meursault demonstrates that his mind has integrated to the extent that it is capable of rejecting any attempt to dissolve the absurdist tension. All of a sudden, this apparently simpleminded individual gathers together all the fragments of his life and mind to form a bold philosophical statement.

But what brings about Meursault's sudden affirmation that everything he has is, truly, everything he desires (Skrimshire 2006: 288)? *The Stranger*'s last pages provide one with an illumined path: At first, the mind that comes to recognize the limits of existence struggles to release itself, but if instead it fervently negates even the subtlest form of escape, the negation finally places it within the limits, enabling one's being to fall into the depths of this life and this universe. From within the limits, one can comprehend the universe from the inside. This, in turn, causes the universe's internal powers and sources of light to awaken; thus, the dark night becomes "alive with signs and stars" (TS, 122).

---

18 Slochower (1969: 293–295) offers a good description of the way in which these two outbursts shatter the inertia of Meursault's life and make him come alive.

This is how absurd walls (MS, 9) turn into absurd freedom (ibid., 49); what appears superficially as a predicament devised by gods, who believed that there could be no greater punishment than futility and eternal repetition (ibid., 115), is transformed by the absurd mind into the happiest of all choices. If one is ready to be condemned, one is no longer condemned. Suffering is not Sisyphus' rock, but rather his imagination that there could be another life at all (ibid., 118–119). Thus, the absurd mind holds an extraordinary power to find liberty "in the oddest of places – even Oran or Hades" (Zaretsky 2013: 37–38) – or prison, for that matter. If, in response to Nietzsche's harrowing thought-experiment,[19] it can sanctify that eternal repetition – if indeed the only other life it envisioned were one where it could remember this life (TS, 120) – the "divorce between man and his life, the actor and his setting" would finally be mended (MS, 5). The life that was given becomes the life that is chosen, and the mind becomes unified with the experience.[20]

An uninterrupted awareness of the limits releases human consciousness from its prison while still being in it. In actuality, the more the limits press in from all sides, the greater the opportunity for liberation. Limits, *The Stranger* tells us, make us conscious, wake us up to the "Why?", encourage us to overcome nihilism, and lead us to deliberately choose and accept our life. Their presence does not weaken the life-force, but rather enhances it, making us "ready to live it all again" (TS, 122).

Yet, this relaxation into the limits of human existence also opens a window onto a type of experience that is briefly introduced on the final pages of both *The Stranger* and *The Myth*. As Meursault calms down after the chaplain's departure, he falls asleep only to wake up with the stars in his face; he is then flooded by the sounds and smells of the earth,[21] and a tide of nature's "wondrous peace" flows through him (TS, 122). While separating from a world that no longer means anything to him, he opens himself to the "gentle indifference of the world" (ibid., 122) and, with genuine

---

19 Several scholars have identified the imprint of Nietzsche's eternal recurrence in this part of the text. See, for example, Golomb 2005: 130, and Scherr 2014: 182.

20 This does not relieve the longing altogether, since Sisyphus' rock consists of both the limit and the longing; it is, after all, the very tension itself.

21 Including "salt air," which represents the sea and unity.

happiness, finds the universe "much like myself – so like a brother, really" (ibid., 122–123). Correspondingly, *The Myth* concludes with a statement that as Sisyphus unites with his limited fate, the godless universe is no longer "sterile nor futile," its now welcome silence allowing the countless "little voices of the earth" to arise and each atom and mineral flake of his stone and mountain to form a world unto itself (MS, 119). These poetic descriptions indicate that the feeling of the universe from the inside may lead to an absurd form of cosmic union.

Whereas the most fundamental experience of the absurd originates from the rift between one's consciousness and life (MS, 5), those cosmic perceptions show one that by fully accepting the strangeness – the impenetrable mystery of oneself and the universe (ibid., 19) – the mind attains an odd kind of intimacy with the world, which goes some way toward healing this essential rift. Both mind and cosmos, knower and known, become, so to speak, brothers in strangeness, bathing in the same unknowable silent waters.[22] "Making a home in one's homelessness" brings about a revelation that one is tied to creation as much as one remains forever a stranger to it (Skrimshire 2006: 289).

This unexpected "harmonious bond" with the universe is uncovered "despite or because of this absurdity" (Golomb 2005: 130). Paradoxically, those who attempt to make the unreasonable world known and familiar, as well as those who strive to transcend it, are the true strangers and outsiders, and, thus, Meursault alone is the "one who is actually at home" (ibid., 130). At the end of the novel, we realize that imposing on oneself the limit of knowing can bring the mind closer to creation and that strangeness does not necessarily mean estrangement. On the contrary, those capable of feeling the universe from the inside have the ears to hear the earth's own voice of depth and meaning.

In light of this interpretation, one can observe that *The Stranger* delineates a clear roadmap of the evolution of the absurd mind. At first, an unformed consciousness meets with the reality of death, the "why?" begins

---

22 The lyrical meditations of Camus' *Noces* contain similar experiences of unity with nature. For instance: "I felt a small part of that force on which I was drifting, then very much part of it, and finally fused with it" (quoted in Dunwoodie 2007: 150–151).

to surface, and it is urged toward a lucid recognition of its predicament. It wrongly resorts to nihilism, which does not even provide relief. Then it takes it upon itself to enter the cosmic cell to confront its limits. In a sincere act of sober humility, it enters an intense process of negation and renunciation – rejecting all hope, all human answers, any release from the tension between longing and fulfillment, and even worldly pleasures. It constantly shifts between acceptance and revolt, until it attains a climax of revolt, which eliminates hope. Finally, this integrated consciousness enters a profound acceptance of limits, realizing that this acceptance liberates it. Now it experiences itself as both imprisoned and liberated, separate and unified, alienated and intimate, longing and content. Merging into the paradoxical nature of the universe itself, it glimpses an absurdist union, a sharing of the unknowable with the cosmos that illumines life from within.

CHAPTER 2

"If I were a tree": Facing the limits of human existence in *The Myth of Sisyphus*

Meursault's adventure – when properly read as an allegory of "coming to consciousness" that corresponds thematically and imagistically to *The Myth*'s "adventure of the mind" (Manly 1964: 321) – proves the recognition of the existence of limits to be a potentially redeeming realization in human life. *The Myth of Sisyphus*, published less than a year after *The Stranger*, advances more confidently and explicitly along the road paved by the novel, allowing both the symbolic and the concrete to transform into the universal and the metaphysical. Though still cautiously described as a personal account (MS, 1), and written in a "poetic style and emotional tone" (Manly 1964: 321), Camus clearly intends to translate Meursault's intuitive and semi-conscious choices into both epistemological and methodological terms; to make clear, philosophically, what he does and why.

Both creations explore a possible mental awakening as a result of a direct encounter between the human mind and the "ultimate realities" (ibid., 321). Yet the awakening offered by the two works is an ironic one: Rather than a transcendent release, they demonstrate how such an encounter can redeem us by reinforcing the limits of human existence and by throwing us – human beings – back on ourselves. In *The Myth*, the obscure representations of such ultimate realities – like a mother's death or a tormenting sun – are replaced with broader, conceptual limits, such as death, knowing, meaning, separation, and repetition. The method, however, is the same: Camus insists on confining himself to the cosmic prison cell, which by now has transformed into the more abstract "absurd walls" (MS, 9), and vehemently rejecting any way out.

Having examined *The Stranger*'s absurd landscape in the previous chapter, it is time to bring to the fore the concept of the absurd as it is more coherently presented in *The Myth of Sisyphus*. Our first step will be to observe how *The Myth* introduces absurdity as a dynamic paradox of living within the limits of existence. I will then offer a critical analysis of Camus' assertion that the experience of the absurd limit results from a collision between humans and the cosmos. In opposition to this metaphysics, I shall argue that it is human consciousness itself that produces absurdity, regardless of the conditions that surround it. In the chapter's second half, I will outline Camus' five untraversable limits – again emphasizing the very existence of a self-transcendent, observing consciousness as the source of our absurd condition.

The paradox of living within the limits

"The absurd does not liberate; it binds," Camus declares (MS, 65), and, faithful to the reality he has come to acknowledge, he devotes many pages of this slim essay to a philosophical attack in the name of the barriers of existence. "This limitation leads me to myself," Camus writes, echoing Karl Jaspers' exclamation, clarifying that they both start in "those waterless deserts where thought reaches its confines," yet drift apart as soon as Jaspers begins to waver with an eagerness to flee those confines (ibid., 8). After all, the "real effort is to stay there" and to "examine closely the odd vegetation of those distant regions" (ibid., 8). For him, what the truth-seeking mind – whether it is religious, philosophical, or scientific – cannot endure is the steadfast recognition of human limits without succumbing to the temptation to try to smash them.

Manav (2013: 132) concludes her investigation into *The Myth* by arguing that "Camus' philosophy of the absurd is that of limitations" in that "it respects the tension of the absurd." Indeed, betraying this lucid recognition – the realization defined by Heidegger as the "finite and limited character of human existence," which is "more primordial than man himself" (MS, 22) – implies turning our back on the absurd, which is by nature an unresolvable tension. The awakening of one's consciousness, which is inaugurated by the sense of the absurd, can only take place when one negates all hope of transcending absurd limits and instead probes them and faces them directly, with a determined wish to clarify them (Sagi 1994: 281).

Camus tirelessly hones the metaphysical borders in the same way that Nietzsche, his predecessor in spirit, did.[1] For this purpose, he applies a methodology that is, he feels, in the very nature of the absurd – recognizing one's path by "discovering the paths that stray from it" (MS, 110). If one wishes to fully know the prison cell, all one needs to do is negate the various attempts to escape it, or, more accurately, the attempts to move beyond its well-defended walls

The Camusean understanding of thinking clearly is to "know that thought itself is limited" and, thus, "to think in part against thought" (Carroll 2007: 60). Throughout the essay's first 48 pages, Camus persistently develops his thinking against thought, establishing a comprehensive negation,[2] while assuring his reader again and again that his interest lies not in discovering the absurd, but rather in the consequences of this discovery (MS, 14). Since the absurd is a given – the "metaphysical state of the conscious man" (ibid., 38) – the only question is "how far is one to go to elude nothing" (ibid., 14). Is it possible and bearable to live with such an uninterrupted recognition of the limits of human experience (ibid., 48)? Nevertheless, he insists that even the consequences must spring directly from this method of persistence (ibid., 36, 51).

A major part of his methodology of negation is employed in opposition to existentialist thought. This should not lead us to conclude that *The Myth* was "explicitly written against existentialists" (Aronson 2017: 7).[3] Rather, Camus' reason for being more particularly critical of their leap beyond the limits of existence is that he clearly recognizes that they share with him the same "spiritual landscapes" and hear the same "cry that terminates their

---

1 To Camus, Nietzsche was the only one who lived up to his own monk-like standards of philosophical abstinence, daring to derive the "extreme consequences of an aesthetic of the absurd" and attaining "a sterile and conquering lucidity and an obstinate negation of any supernatural consolation" (MS, 133).

2 Camus seems to be content with his process of negation, since on page 49 he declares, "Now the main thing is done," and moves on to discuss its implications.

3 See also Foley (2008: 1) who similarly argues that Camus' essay was intended as a "critique of existentialism."

itinerary" (MS, 27). It is a profound sense of kinship that leads him to decide to continue on from the point where they have stopped (ibid., 8). Like them, he too starts with the "initial absurd premise of existentialism" (Foley 2008: 3), which is the sobering recognition of human limits, but he observes that their negation process has remained somewhat incomplete – not as a result of some philosophical feeble-mindedness, but simply because it is too unnerving to maintain such a position "under that stifling sky" (MS, 27). It is in their responses to the absurd reality that they have all failed, Camus concludes, since they "refuse to accept the conclusions that follow from their own premises"; sooner or later, they seek to "appeal to something beyond the limits of the human condition" (Aronson 2017: 8).

Camus is perfectly aware that such a desert-like, deadly climate inevitably produces its own fata morganas, "mirages of escape and salvation" (Carroll 2007: 58). More than the specific strategies employed by each – be it Kierkegaard, Dostoevsky, Chestov, Scheler, or Kafka – he pointedly identifies the underlying frailty of their philosophies: that they are "steeped in a vast hope" (MS, 131). "Within the limits of the human condition," he asks in his discussion of Kafka's betrayal of the absurd, "what greater hope than the hope that allows an escape from that condition?" (ibid., 131).

Hope, as a single, irrational force, is the error Camus is determined to avoid (Aronson 2017: 3) and that which his negation strives to obliterate, since it is the betrayal of limit and, therefore, life's nemesis. Aronson (ibid., 3–4) points out that here Camus relies on Nietzsche's discussion of Pandora's Box in *Human, All Too Human*. After "all the evils of humankind" have been "let loose on the world by Zeus," the one last evil, hope, has remained hidden within the box. What humans see as their "greatest good," Zeus considered the "greatest source of trouble." Hope is the imagination of an overcoming of limits, a fantasy of a different, less limited existence, or at least one in which the burden of existence – the burden of living with limits – is removed from one's shoulders. It looks beyond life for something else that will "transcend it, refine it, give it a meaning and betray it" (MS, 7), and, thus, it leads humans to "minimize the value of life" (Aronson 2017: 4). With the cessation of all hope and the lucid acknowledgment of life's contours, what seemed to be stifling becomes life-enhancing and the intrinsic value and beauty of life are uncovered, not because life is unlimited in any sense, but truly *because* it is limited.[4]

Hope strives to dissolve the walls of the prison cell and to run away from the only life we have. However, the other extreme, that of despair and the submissive acceptance of the cell's bars, is just as debilitating and "equally illusory" (Carroll 2007: 59), since it frees humans from the healthy tension that causes them to constantly develop responses that increase, rather than decrease, life's vitality in them. Herein lies much of what makes Camus' absurdism more complex and sophisticated than that of his existential predecessors: the contention that even consenting to absurdity and ceasing to rebel against it robs the absurd of any meaning (Smith 2011: 3).

Bowker (2008: 170) claims that "the ambivalence of the absurd entails an ambivalent attitude toward absurdity, itself." Elsewhere, he refers to Cruickshank, who argued that *The Myth* moves from the basic contrasts of Camus' earlier works – for instance, between life and death, or knowledge and the unknowable – to the "discordancy of a paradox," which makes it far less easy to live (ibid., 138–139). This paradox turns the limit into a juncture of unending and engaging tension, between the aspiration to overcome limits and the conscious acceptance of them. Indeed, human existence is a contradiction without relief; being tension itself, its dynamism and evolution are the result of that friction and strife. Thus, the limit as a meeting point of opposing yet balancing forces can be considered the "holy equation" of human life.

Of course, remaining within the limits contradicts human instinct. If one found oneself imprisoned, one would obviously seek a way out. It is, after all, only natural that, upon establishing in oneself the truth of absurdity, one should aspire to "escape the universe of which [one] is the creator" (MS, 30). The individual would refuse to "be consumed by the absurd" and would strive to "limit its power over him [or her]" (Skrimshire 2006: 297–298). Since absurd walls are undissolvable, and yet the instinct is undeniable, this imprints in humans, rather than Nietzsche's "will to power," a "will to resist" – "even or especially when resistance appears hopeless"

---

4   This can be interestingly compared to Eagleton's concept of authentic hope (2015). Indeed, Eagleton deploys the term in a way that could strike us as quite close to Sisyphus' joy (MS, 117).

(Carroll 2007: 54). This marks yet another limit – that of "individual re-sistance to the human condition itself" (ibid., 54). Humans are doomed to wish to try to overcome the limits, or at least to imagine that they have succeeded in doing so. Hence, even the existentialists' various leaps, criti-cized by Camus, are still absurd; in the belief that such leaps have solved the paradox, they actually reinstate it intact (MS, 63). Just like everyone else, the existentialists are akin to a "blind man eager to see who knows that the night has no end" (ibid., 119).

Having introduced the concept of limits in *The Myth*, let us turn to a more focused discussion of the true origin of our absurd clash with the limits of existence.

Where are those absurd walls?

It is Camus' contention that absurd walls exist neither in human con-sciousness nor in the universe, but at the meeting point between the two. Pölzler (2014: 92) identifies three features that make up Camus' absurdism: The absurd is a relation; the relation is one of contradiction and divorce, and its relating parts are the subject's quest and the objective world. While this is indeed *The Myth*'s metaphysical worldview, I believe that we should question the human/cosmos collision as the true origin of the absurd experience. Here I side with Nagel (1971: 716–727), who accepts Camus' essential feeling that life is absurd, but argues that Camus did not adequately explain why this is so.

By taking a deeper and more logically convincing look at the source of the absurd, Nagel reveals something more intrinsic in the human condition that is absurd. First, he demonstrates that the conditions that are assumed to create the absurd predicament in human life can be easily refuted; he does this by employing several simple thought-experiments (somewhat resembling those of science fiction films) that imagine other conditions that would also sustain the feeling of the absurd: for instance, a universe in which what we did now would matter in a million years (ibid., 716); a universe in which we lived forever or were far bigger than a "speck of dust" (ibid., 717), or a universe whose meaning and purpose were fully disclosed (ibid., 721). Then, opposing Camus' postulation that the absurd arises in us due to the indifferent and silent world in which we live – which suggests that a different world *might* "satisfy those demands" – Nagel writes, "There does not appear to be any conceivable world (containing us) about which unsettleable doubts could not arise," and concludes that absurdity derives from a "collision within ourselves" (ibid., 721–722).

There is at least one instance in *The Myth* of Camus seemingly contradicting his own human/cosmos premise and identifying our internal collision as the true source of absurdity: when he states that "there can be no absurd outside the human mind" (MS, 29). Another significant remark, which makes a similar allusion, will be discussed in the next section. Further developing Nagel's line of thought and Camus' own undeveloped deviation, we can deduce that the specific limits with which Camus is concerned are not necessarily the crux of the absurdist problem. Limits, as well as our rebellion against them, would appear in any imaginable universe. Given that the absurd does not derive from the mind's relations with the particular limits of a specific world, one may logically conclude that the absurd is a condition that we would take with us to any universe, regardless of the conditions of that universe. It is ingrained in the very nature of human consciousness, and the reason it seems to appear at the meeting point between mind and universe is simply that the human mind is the only agent known to us that could actually encounter the cosmos in a complex subject–object relationship.

That said, I shall still describe in this chapter the limits of this particular universe, as outlined by Camus, for two reasons. First and foremost, a close inspection of *The Myth*'s metaphysical limits further illustrates Nagel's insight into the absurd – so long as the experience of these limits is correctly viewed as clashes between different viewpoints within ourselves. Secondly, an overview of Camus' limits will serve us well in analyzing the films, which confront humans, aliens and A.I. alike with such limits in ways that drive them to test their own inner boundaries, as well as their preconceived notions about the universe's limits.

Accordingly, I have chosen as my starting point a limit that Camus' scholars have focused on significantly less and that, in my opinion, truly captures the origin of absurdism in the nature of human consciousness itself. Even if all other conditions were different, this limit could not be removed because, in its absence, the human component of Camus' absurdist equation would no longer exist.

The limit of separation

"If I were a tree among trees, a cat among animals," writes Camus, "this life would have a meaning or rather this problem would not arise; for I should belong to this world. I should *be* this world to which I am now opposed by my whole consciousness and my whole insistence upon familiarity. This ridiculous reason is what sets me in opposition to all creation" (MS, 49–50). Shortly thereafter, he asks, "What constitutes the basis of that conflict, of that break between the world and my mind, but the awareness of it?" (ibid., 50). These lines, suffused with what Camus himself calls "nostalgia for unity" verging on a craving for "self-dehumanization," reveal that the real object of his demand for meaning and knowing is to "become one with the world" and to attain a "world without difference" (Bowker 2008: 144–145). For him, when "man has an idea of a better world than this," better "does not mean different, it means unified" (ibid., 147–148).

One cannot ignore the fact that the term "nostalgia" hints at a state of unity that once was and to which one cannot return, as if "nature, itself, rejected us" and "spat us out of the ocean and onto the shore" (ibid., 166). As Bowker shows, Camus' early work and short fiction are filled with "an erotic desire for a natural union," often expressed through insatiable sexual imagery: "It was neither I nor the world that counted," Camus reflects, "but solely the harmony and silence that gave birth to the love between us" (ibid., 148). During such brief moments of fusion with the world, he most certainly did not feel the uprootedness and alienness of the absurd, negated by the inhuman beauty of nature (MS, 4–5, 12–13). Yet the limit of separation dictates that such a union could never be realized fully and cathartically and that any seemingly everlasting intimacy with the natural world must eventually dissipate. Camus is then violently "thrust back upon himself" (Bowker 2008: 149), whereupon he realizes that nostalgia's existence does not imply its satisfaction and that Parmenides' "reality of the One" already holds within it its contradiction of difference and diversity (MS, 16).

This limit is critical, since it marks the primary condition for the very existence of the absurd: If we were trees, we would be creation itself and thus untouched by absurdity, but, as humans, we are separate from creation and that is how the absurd creeps in. Absurdity only exists in humans, but why? In what way is a human not a tree? It is their added layer of consciousness, their capacity to not only be alive but also to *know* that they are alive. Sagi (1994: 280) puts it simply: "Were human beings bereft of consciousness, they could not sense the absurd." As a result of this capacity, humans are endowed with an external perspective on the particular form of their lives, and thus they are able to "step back and reflect on the process," ask "whether what they are doing is worth while," and even survey themselves with "detached amazement" (Nagel 1971: 719–720). Consciousness, a perspective "broader than we can occupy in the flesh," makes us "pure spectators of our lives" who can transcend ourselves in thought (ibid., 725).

This dual existence of the participant in life and the observer of life in one unit is both a blessing and a curse – a curse because it creates an inevitable and essentially agonizing distance from the stream of life. Unlike the "tree among trees" and "cat among cats" human consciousness quickly splits the universe into a complex, self-reflective relationship between subject and object, observer and observed, and since the absurd collision occurs at the meeting point between the apparent subject and the apparent object, this constitutes the basis of the conflict: The absurd lies between life and the consciousness of life.[5] It is this consciousness that brings humans

---

5 This may be somewhat similar to Sartre's concept of dissociation: "The never completed split in consciousness attempted by consciousness in reflection"; a split between the only seemingly separate parts of the reflective consciousness and the "consciousness reflected-on" (Sartre 2003: 651).

to the "threshold of the alienation experience," to the feeling of being a "stranger" (Sagi 2002: 12).

Smith (2011: 2) quotes Jean Grenier, Camus' teacher and friend, who wrote, "We are not in the world, this thought is the genesis of philosophizing," and remarks, "yet on the other hand 'being-in-the-world' and Mitsein are key concepts of phenomenology. How are these apparently mutually exclusive positions reconciled?" Indeed, if there were a spiritual dimension and we perceived ourselves as souls or spirits who merely visit the physical universe, that strangeness would be justified, but in the absurdist universe there can be nothing besides the visible world of phenomena from which consciousness is inherently inseparable.[6] In light of the fact that we cannot *not* be the cosmos – for consciousness can only consist of the same elements that compose the rest of creation – we should feel most at home in such a universe. This paradox causes human consciousness to intuit that there should be an underlying unity, which it is unable to achieve and can only long for.

"This mind and this world," writes Camus sorrowfully, "straining against each other without being able to embrace each other" (MS, 39). That is the essence of the absurd: the unreasonable gap between subject and object, the existence of both in a single being. It is the awkward feeling that we do not belong to a creation to which we should belong and with which we should even experience a harmonious unity. Where natural union fails, "metaphysical thought" seeks to compensate and to offer a union of its own (Bowker 2008: 156): Through philosophy, religion and science, it attempts to make the universe known and familiar and, thus, to attain a unity of observer and observed. But, for Camus, this is a lost battle, since "all the knowledge on earth will give me nothing to assure me that this world is mine" (MS, 18).

---

6 This is compatible with the way Buber describes the Aristotelian view that "man is a thing among these things of the universe" (Sagi 2002: 10). Another way to look at it is that consciousness always appears together with the world; thus, both exist as an inseparable unit. See Hume's (2015) straightforward description: "I never can catch myself at any time without a perception, and never can observe any thing but the perception."

This strangeness extends to one's relationship with oneself. "To exist is to be a stranger to oneself and to the world" (Skrimshire 2006: 288). That is because we are also aware of ourselves, and that awareness creates a distance between "I" and "myself." Consequently, it is a stranger who "comes to meet us in a mirror"[7] and we encounter a "familiar yet alarming brother [...] in our photographs" (MS, 13), and as we search within ourselves for this self, we find that it is undefinable, "nothing but water slipping through [our] fingers" (ibid., 17). Hence, the Socratic dictum, "Know Thyself," is more a moral value, utterly inefficacious when it comes to actual reality, in which even one's heart is not one's own (ibid., 17).

While this internal divide instigates humans to struggle for unity, Bowker (2008: 141) claims that at the heart of the struggle lies an ambivalence within consciousness itself "between unity and individuality, wholeness and independence." Like Nagel, he feels that Camus' absurd is a collision within ourselves, manifesting in this case as the tension between two opposing desires: the longing to lose oneself to attain union, and the "desire for the self," which strives to protect one's limits of individuality and separate consciousness (ibid., 150, 160). In this sense, it is not the indifferent world that refuses our plea for union, but our very own opposing desire to return to our body "even with all of its limits and frailties" (ibid., 163). It is consciousness that aspires to remain in that tension, "neither absolutely unified nor absolutely separate" (ibid., 169).

The limits of knowing, meaning, death and repetition

The unique capacity of human consciousness to stand apart from the rest of creation, to stick out, as it were, and rise above its mass of energy and matter, first engenders the limit of separation and, quickly thereafter, all

---

7 In this line we can find an echo of the metaphor of the mirror in *The Stranger*, which appears twice: once when Meursault's own reflection is absent and once, near the end of the novel, when he attains, through the awakening of his awareness in light of absurd limits, a unification with the "stranger" in the mirror (TS, 24, 81).

other limits as well. It could even be said that we are a consciousness that is aware, before anything else, of its own limits; torn between the "urge towards unity" and the "clear vision" of the walls enclosing it (MS, 21). As soon as consciousness awakes, it finds itself in prison.

I shall briefly describe the four other limits that arise from this very same source.

The limit of knowing

As mentioned above, when the "mind's deepest desire" (MS, 15) to "return" to natural unity goes unfulfilled, it takes the form of the wish to make the world fully known and familiar through reason and knowledge: "To understand is above all to unify" (ibid., 15). The mind exerts all its self-reflective capacities to reduce the universe to the human and to stamp it with its "seal" (ibid., 15–16), seeking to achieve a "rational unity" by bringing together everything "under one comprehensive system" (Smith 2011: 2). What awaits it is the bitter realization that its inability to "impose its patterns on everything" is not some "relative handicap," which may one day be eradicated by the progress of science, but an "absolute limitation," which the universe's "ultimate unintelligibility" delineates (ibid., 2–3).

As the "intellect confronts the limits of the rational" and realizes that it is "simply incapable of performing the task asked of it," its impotence does not lead it to humble acceptance (Bowker 2008: 147). Rather, it begins to cheat, either by "idealizing its ignorance" or insisting on "imposing form upon a world without form" (ibid., 167). Camus sees through the mind's attempts to evade or conquer the world's undefeatable chaos, describing the history of human thought as the "history of its successive regrets and impotences" (MS, 17) and arguing that intelligence's grand enterprise only "tells me in its way that this world is absurd" (ibid., 18–19).

Yet, since Camus' limits are also unresolvable tensions, he does not "put himself against science and philosophy," by "dismissing the claims of all forms of rational analysis" (Aronson 2017: 5). Unlike irrationalists, who maintain that reason is useless, he tries to "rationally understand the limits of reason" (ibid., 6).[8] It is not that we, either as individuals or as a collective human species, can know nothing; it is rather that we cannot know everything. Therefore, Camus' main concern is to ensure that our insatiable demand for meaning, order, and unity does not lead us to aspire to transcend those limits to "pursue the impossible" (ibid., 6). Nonetheless, in the spirit of Nagel's thought-experiments, one should ask: If all of the mysteries of the universe in which we lived were unconditionally disclosed to us, would the disquieting feeling that our life is absurd be entirely eliminated?

The limit of meaning

The duality of human consciousness, which divides us into an observer and a participant, naturally endows us with the capacity to "step back and reflect on the process" and to ask "whether what [we] are doing is worth while" (Nagel 1971: 719–720). Hence, we feel driven to rectify the broken unity by gaining the ultimate, but impossible, knowledge: the "why" of our existence. The problem, after all, is not that the world remains unintelligible, but that it "remains unintelligible in ways meaningful to humankind" (Foley 2008: 7). Put simply, it is not that, as humanity, we want to know everything; rather, we want to obtain that part of cosmic knowledge that could shed light on the sense of our life.

Faithful to his own principle of absurd tension, Camus is not content with simply asserting that life is meaningless. Instead, he writes, "I don't know whether this world has a meaning that transcends it. But I know that I do not know that meaning and that it is impossible for me just now to know it" (MS, 49). Any meaning outside the human condition would mean nothing "within the limits of my condition" (ibid., 49). Thus, what we confront is not a reality of meaninglessness, but, again, the inability

---

8 Indeed, this is the basis for much of his criticism of the existentialists, who elude absurd tension in a more sophisticated way than the rationalists do – by "denying even whatever little reason is in man" (Manav 2013: 129). See, for instance, Camus' criticism of Chestov, who deemed reason useless only to replace it with "something beyond reason": "To an absurd mind," Camus writes, "reason is useless and there is nothing beyond reason" (MS, 34).

to know in absolute terms, as well as the irrelevance of such an ultimate meaning to the actuality of human life.

Several scholars (e.g. Ayer 1946; Bowker 2008; Pölzler 2014) have argued that Camus' conception of meaning – its demand that everything be explained or nothing and its insistence on a perfect and continuous clarity – is overly ambitious and exaggerated, and thus the limits of knowing and meaning are more a matter of unrealistic expectations. Nagel (1971: 721–722) adds that even a universe that laid bare the purpose of our existence would be found dissatisfactory by us and would arouse our doubts. Hence, the true problem is that humans presuppose that there must be some hidden meaning, and that, if found, all absurdity would be resolved. But such criticism overlooks the fact that Camus neither believed that such a meaning could ever be known nor expected that human yearning could ever be truly fulfilled.

This creates a vital friction between our impulse to keep on asking about the meaning of life and the inevitable moments when we, like Sisyphus, must "see our answers tumble back down" (Aronson 2017: 2). The absurdity is even more acute in the case of the meaning of life, since this question is a matter of "eternal immediacy" (Zaretsky 2013: 12). We should remember that The Myth itself is a philosophical battle that is initially incited by the insistence not upon answering, but rather upon responding to this "most urgent of questions" (MS, 2). Indeed, it is a question that gives rise to a dynamism of spirit, not because it is brought to the fore, but because an authentic encounter with the limit it poses is the key to a life filled with a sort of built-in meaning: a life that is worth living without any external justification. In the end, Camus concludes that life will be lived "all the better if it has no meaning" (MS, 51), since, in such a life, the distance between the observer and the participant – initially caused by the dynamic of meaning-seeking self-contemplation – is diminished, replaced by a unity of experiencer and experience.

The limit of death

This limit, the authentic way to face it and its major contribution to the process of self-integration in light of the absurd[9] are best demonstrated in *The Stranger*, most notably in its final chapter. At first, one may regard Meursault as a special case, a murderer condemned to death, but Camus makes it clear, after stripping the symbol of the guillotine of its particularity, that everyone is "the man condemned to death" (MS, 53). "Whether it was now or twenty years from now," Meursault acknowledges, "I would still be the one dying" (TS, 114). For everyone, "the trouble with the guillotine" is that one has "no chance at all" (ibid., 111), and, for that reason, "the only thing a man could be truly interested in" is execution (ibid., 110). An even more gruesome realization is that the "guillotine is on the same level as the man approaching it"; thus, one does not go, as one would hope, "right up into the sky" (ibid., 112). This makes death a "closed door" rather than a "gateway to another life" (Aronson 2017: 4). On the other hand, the "conscious certainty of a death without hope" is where true wisdom lies (ibid., 3).

For Camus, death is the "most obvious absurdity" (MS, 57) and, therefore, the most tangible and undeniable limit of human existence. However, it is not the general awareness of human mortality – the unconvincing death of others – that brings an individual into a "confrontation with the absurd condition," but rather one's own personal mortality (Foley 2008: 6). Although "everyone lives as if no one knew," since all we know is life and consciousness (MS, 14), there are instances in which one recognizes that the "tomorrow" for which one was longing and toward which one was rushing has to be traveled to its end, where life's limit awaits (ibid., 12). An individual builds his or her life meticulously and cautiously only to realize that all this building culminates in disintegration. Indeed, it is the limit of death that poses, in the most intimidating and urgent way, the question of whether life is worth living at all.

---

9 Even more absurd is the fact that self-integration increases in the face of the threat of self-dissolution.

However, Nagel (1971: 717) argues that an average lifetime of seventy years would be simply "infinitely absurd" if it lasted forever. It is certainly conceivable that the lives of vampires, or, for that matter, any kind of physically eternal being, might be steeped in absurdity, perhaps to an even greater degree due to the enhanced sense of pointlessness and repetition. This raises the possibility that the absurdity of this limit lies elsewhere. As observed in our consideration of the limit of separation, a tree does not possess an observing consciousness that reflects on its impending cessation even when it is perfectly healthy and vital, whereas humans experience a peculiar tension between their witnessing consciousness and their dying body. Meursault, for instance, is stunned when he imagines, in his prison cell, the ending of his heartbeat, "this sound which had been with me for so long," yet he keeps on trying to picture that exact moment (TS, 112–113). Hence, it is not so much the fact that we are going to die that constitutes the absurdity of death, but rather the fact that we know that we are going to die. The gap between consciousness and life, which coexist in one body, produces a form that observes its own process of coming apart. It disengages mind from body, giving rise to the condition of a perishable body and a mind that cannot conceive of its own non-existence.

The limit of repetition

Repetition is another undeniable and easily perceptible limit that can enable humans to become "fully conscious" and "sense the absurd" (Aronson 2017: 6). It is the recognition that our being is tied to mechanical habits, from the tedious and cyclical rhythms of routine to personality patterns, which we cannot break. We "continue making the gestures commanded by existence," enduring the "insane character of that daily agitation" (MS, 4). In such a universe, in which "nothing is possible but everything is given" (ibid., 58), we come to realize that our belief in the choice to be ourselves and our hope that something in our life "can be directed" shatter in the face of the absurd truth that "there is no future" (ibid., 56). This limit instills our every experience with a taint of futility, and any desperate attempt to "move more quickly" leads us nowhere (Zaretsky 2013: 12–13).

Futility is at the heart of the Sisyphean myth, in which Camus envisions eternal repetition – straining to accomplish nothing – as the "unspeakable penalty" that all humans must endure (MS, 116). Zaretsky (2013: 38–39) emphasizes that Sisyphus' torment has little to do with physical exertion; the true suffering lies in the mind "challenged by the endlessly repetitive nature of the task." What strikes us at first as a metaphysical fable quickly transforms into everyday life, if we only consider the "phenomenon of finality rebounding like a ball," which is "work in order to eat" and "eat in order to work" (Skrimshire 2006: 291). This is what Pölzler (2014: 93) refers to as the feeling of meaninglessness caused by doing things for the sake of other things, with nothing that is "worth pursuing for itself" to give direction to our daily gestures.

Yet, in a way similar to the limit of death, it is worth clarifying that repetition in itself is not absurd; it is only the fact that a witnessing consciousness observes that repetition and is powerless to escape it that ignites absurdity in us. Nagel (1971: 725) points out that in the absence of self-transcendence, a mouse is not absurd, since it lacks the capacity that would enable it to see that it is "only a mouse." But if self-consciousness did arise in it, its life would become absurd, since it would then struggle with the paradox of knowing it is a mouse and leading its "meagre yet frantic life" without being able to rise above its own programming. This echoes Camus' point concerning Oedipus – that his suffering begins only as soon as he becomes conscious of his predetermined and unalterable fate (MS, 118). Thus, the deeper nature of the limit of repetition is the struggle of a consciousness that experiences essential freedom, derived from its awareness, imagination and doubt, with the fixed and arbitrary patterns of life and its own personality, in which it is entrapped. In Nagel's words, it is the "dragooning of an unconvinced transcendent consciousness into the service of an immanent, limited enterprise like a human life" (1971: 726).[10]

---

10 In his critical essay on *The Stranger*, Brombert (1948: 120) mentions that "that is what Sartre calls the divorce between the physical and the spiritual nature of man."

As previously stated, the complex, paradoxical and inherently absurd nature of human consciousness would appear in any imagined universe, including one that might better fulfill our expectations or one with a different, seemingly "freer" prison cell for humans. This is because the mind component in the universe/mind equation would remain unchanged. The eternal interplay of limit and longing would, even in improved conditions, give rise to its havoc of contradiction. This, as we shall see in Part II, will constitute a salient insight in our discussion of science fiction films, which, by their very nature, alter the conditions of the universe and entertain different modes and forms of existence in the cosmos, thus challenging the exclusivity of the absurd experience as we know it.

What remains unexplored in my consideration of Camus' philosophy is the range of proper and improper human responses once one has fully acknowledged the inescapable tangibility of these absurd limits. This topic shall be addressed in the following chapter.

CHAPTER 3

"A strange form of love": Responding to the limits of human existence in *The Myth of Sisyphus* and *The Rebel*

It was in 1938 – around two years before embarking on his journey of *The Myth of Sisyphus* – that Camus received, as the book reviewer for the newspaper *Alger républicain*, two thin books by a young and as yet unknown writer who was wrestling with the absurd (Zaretsky 2013: 15–16). One can see why these two creations by Jean-Paul Sartre – *The Wall*, a short story collection, and *Nausea*, a novel – would have piqued Camus' attention. Indeed, as someone who had taken it upon himself, as early as 1936, to become an explicator of absurdity, Camus found the stories compelling, but deemed them incapable of providing more than a mere depiction of the "world's oppressive density," thus culminating in "existential solipsism" (ibid., 15). Camus wrote that since the realization that life is absurd has been a truth that almost all great minds have used as their starting point, it was not the discovery that interested him, but rather "the consequences and rules for action" drawn from it (Camus, quoted in Manav 2013: 127).

Was *The Myth of Sisyphus* Camus' answer to Sartre's solipsism, or, at least, an answer to his own pressing need, which he found disappointingly unsatiated by Sartre's stories? To a certain degree, perhaps. After all, the essay's very first page announces – almost as a direct continuation of that literary review – that whereas the absurd has thus far been considered a conclusion, in this case it will serve as a point of departure (MS, 1). Since the absurd is a given as the most elementary phase of philosophical discovery, the real question is what one should *conclude*: "How far is one to go to elude nothing?" (MS, 14). Faithful to this exigency, after many stormy pages filled with persistent negation and an ever tightening delineation of the "absurd walls" of the human condition, he leaps to his one true agenda: an exploration of consequences bearing the title "absurd freedom" (ibid., 49).

The consequences of one's lucid recognition of the absurd – also explored in *Caligula*, *The Stranger*, and, much later, *The Rebel* – can be thought of as the full range of human responses. The objective of this chapter is to examine the variety of possible responses offered by Camus in these works; some – like suicide, murder, nihilism, hope, and renunciation – are vehemently rejected by Camus as timid reactions that allow one to avoid walking the path to its end, and some – like acceptance, revolt, freedom, passion,[1] and human solidarity – are commended as pathways toward human flourishing in light of the absurd. It is significant to note that for Camus, none of these responses are merely theoretical; as Aronson puts it, Camus deems it obvious, at least within the context of his own inquiry, that the "primary result of philosophy is action," since the question that such reactions strive to answer is the "life-and-death problem of whether and how to live" in the deadly climate of the absurd (2017: 5). Thus, all are modes of *action* that spring from *recognition*. Yet, what it is exactly that causes such modes of action to spring from recognition is a matter of great contention among Camus' scholars, and we should seek to better understand these dynamics before introducing both his negative and positive active responses.

Where do the ethics come from?

A long list of scholars (e.g. Duff and Marshall 1982; Sagi 1994; Foley 2008, and Pölzler 2014) have engaged in the debate over whether Camus' "positive" responses to absurdity are anything more than moral ideals artificially projected onto the bare and plain world uncovered by *The*

---

1 Revolt, freedom and passion are what Camus calls the "three consequences" (MS, 62). Since he chose to tie all three together, I have treated them as one response in this chapter.

Myth – a single human standing alone in an empty, skyless universe.[2] In such a world, the only acceptable moral code is the one that is not separated from God, yet "it so happens" that the absurd man "lives outside that God" (MS, 64–65). Duff and Marshall (1982: 117) argue that *The Myth*'s destructive enterprise was too successful to accommodate any "positive reconstruction of values" and, thus, its "atomistic nihilism" leaves no "logical space" (ibid., 129) for "a more developed moral response" (ibid., 124). Certainly, they claim, *The Myth*'s universe cannot contain – and even resists – Camus' later social and political response to the absurd in *The Rebel* (ibid., 117). Sagi (1994: 278–284) and Pölzler (2014: 91–102), each in their own way, also attempt to resolve this paradox, in which, "without God, values must somehow flow from ordinary human experience" (Sagi 1994: 278). How can a metaphysics of a silent, unreasonable world bring forth, out of nothing, virtues, normative ethical conclusions, and rules for life? Was Camus so terrified of the universe he himself had created that he felt compelled to imbue it with sources of motivation and encouragement, or did Camus the moralist intervene in order to instruct the otherwise lost absurd individual?[3]

To begin with, the perception that *The Myth* is a "stage of nihilistic thought through which any honest thinker must pass" is unjustified (Duff and Marshall 1982; 117). The entire scope of Camus' early works is an impassioned struggle against nihilism, driven by his wish to "transform into a rule of life what was an invitation to death" (MS, 62). Nihilism, as I shall demonstrate later, is a negative response to the absurd, one that Camus vehemently rejects, at least partially because it violates the tension between acceptance and revolt inherent in his definition of absurdity. Thus, *The Myth* is a constructive endeavor just as much as it is destructive; that is, its negation is carefully devised to lead to a new creation. In this sense, it may be proposed that Camus took it upon himself to continue Nietzsche's

---

2 Ironically, Duff and Marshall (1982: 117) use the same argument that Camus employed against Sartre when they criticize Camus for his over-solipsistic metaphysics in *The Myth*.

3 See, for instance, Bronner (1999: 151), whose work aims to establish Camus' enterprise as the creation of a "positive morality, if not a sense of ethics, capable of providing rules for secular living."

declared mission: to go against the tide of mankind's newfound freedom, celebrated by the "liberal-minded unbeliever" who dispensed with the existence of God only to drown in senselessness and insignificance (Hollingdale 1999: 32–33). Nietzsche, like Camus, believed that this freedom meant "not only throwing off a burden but taking on a heavier one in its place" (ibid., 32).

It must be noted, however, that Camus was far from convinced that the Nietzschean experiment was successful in conquering nihilism. While deeply respecting him for not flinching, Camus points out that Nietzsche's rebellion ends in victory over oneself and "asceticism" (TR, 44–45). By promoting the idea that one must unconditionally consent to life as it is, Camus argues, Nietzsche deifies fate and thereby renounces the crucial element of rebellion – "the ethic which refuses to accept the world as it is" (ibid., 47–50). Worse than that, such consent makes the rebel kneel not only before the cosmic will, but also before history – his "yes" to everything includes an acceptance of the existence of evil and murder, preserves the world's injustice, and inhibits important ethical distinctions (ibid., 48–53).

In his 1944 article "Le Pessimisme et le Courage," Camus elucidates his task: to determine whether man "can unaided create his own values" (Camus, quoted in Foley 2008: 1). While he does not believe that "negation encompasses everything," he is certain that it should be the "beginning of everything" (ibid., 173), since it enables one "to make a tabula rasa, on the basis of which it would be possible to construct something" (ibid., 8). Hence, as he further clarified in a 1951 interview, The Myth was not about looking for a doctrine, but rather about finding a method – one that could demonstrate how an unwavering negativity gives rise to a "creative capacity," which makes it possible to "respond positively to the absurd" (ibid., 8).

In Chapter 1, I suggested a reading of The Stranger as a foundational text that can shed light on Camus' "method of persistence" in The Myth. Such a reading might aid us in our effort to tap into the origin of ethics in Sisyphus' universe. In the second part of The Stranger, we find Meursault fervently arresting any possible movement of his thought toward emotional or conceptual release, yet somehow this unyielding resistance – this "methodical doubt" (Camus, quoted in Foley 2008: 8) – transforms into a profound affirmation of life's value (TS, 122). Similarly, Sisyphus, at "the hour of consciousness," beholds the enormity of his tragedy, yet he chooses to unify with it, thus releasing his limited universe from its sterility and illuminating it with the bright colors of positivity (MS, 119). In the end, both creations show that "generous forms of behavior can be engendered even in a world without God" and that negation makes room for the absurd hero to "create his own values" (Camus, quoted in Foley 2008: 4).

This process, which may strike us at first as a logical leap, is indeed an organic growth; an inevitable chain reaction, so to speak, comprising a lucid recognition of the unembellished metaphysical reality and the resulting affirmation and awakening of vital forces within oneself. Hence, it requires no ethical intervention of the kind that systemizes and recommends the ways in which one "ought" to be and live. The emergence of a vital life-force in either Meursault or Sisyphus certainly does not fall into any known categories of virtues, duties, or consequences of actions. It is perhaps closest to eudaemonist virtue ethics – developing virtues because they contribute to our flourishing – with one major difference: Camus' human flourishing takes place as a by-product of an unwavering realization of one's authentic relationship with the universe.

What seemed to some a "certain sleight of hand," which suddenly and unjustifiably embraces a "normative stance, affirming specific values" (Aronson 2017: 9), is really "the actualization of a process of self-knowledge" (Sagi 1994: 282). In fact, the paradox with which many scholars have wrestled exists only so long as we interpret *The Myth* as "an ethical rather than as an ontological existential text"; when it is read purely as a process of self-revelation, one realizes that what sustains its ethics are metaphysical, not ethical, considerations (ibid., 284).

One could say that the sole ethical decision in *The Myth* – the excellent character trait that one ought to cultivate – is Camus' determination to remain faithful to the reality he has discovered: It is the bold insistence to follow up "his ideas to the end"; "to be logical right through, at all costs" (C, 7). The *persistence* would lead, eventually, to the *consequences* – not through formal logic, but more as a leap of the human heart in response to what it beholds, or, less metaphorically, as the direct outcome of a lucid and authentic experiential confrontation (Pölzler 2014: 96). If there are virtues that Camus endorses – such as sincerity, courage, and mental strength – they are not, as Pölzler assumes (ibid., 94–95), worthy "absurd ways of living," but prerequisites for an unswerving and complete realization of the absurd. Such character traits, unlike the Aristotelian virtues, are really philosophical qualities that keep one from succumbing to the instinctual wish to flee absurd reality. Their role is to preserve "an aesthetic of existence, an attitude that refuses lies, the 'sidestepping' of philosophical traditions" (Skrimshire 2006: 289) – in Camus' own words, "a certain kind of personal conduct in which life would confront life as it is and not with daydreams" (Zaretsky 2013: 18).

Camus aims to demonstrate that the discovery of the absurd awakens and integrates the human mind, consequently guiding it – through the lucid recognition that this is truly the only life we have – to fully "affirm human existence" (Sagi 1994: 283). In this respect, the positive responses spring from increased conscious awareness. If they constituted ethical advice, they would not be intrinsically superior to any other suggested responses, including negative ones such as nihilism or suicide. Since, in an amoral, unreasonable world, all responses are born equal, "any response is equally rational" (Duff and Marshall 1982: 127), and so, Camus can no longer claim to have a philosophical justification when he denounces certain responses. Here, too, we find Camus struggling with the very same ethical problem his predecessor-in-spirit, Nietzsche, was grappling with: Having followed "systematic negation," including the destruction of all values, one realizes that "any attempt to apply a standard of values to the world leads finally to a slander on life." It is virtue that now needs justification, since "what should be does not exist" (TR, 39–43). Yet, if we evaluate the responses according to their level of depth and awareness, we may find that the negative responses are the outcome of a superficial insight into the reality of absurdity, whereas the positive responses emerge from a total, unreserved confrontation with it.

Camus' early works – and *The Rebel*, as I shall soon assert – are filled with realizations that lead to realizations. Since the absurd is "an experience that must be lived through" (TR, 4), these are developments that can only be achieved by trial and error, experimenting by actually living in its light. A life such as this, which unflinchingly faces the absurd, can naturally bring the sincere individual to withdraw from erroneous responses and to progress to life-enhancing ones. There are at least four instances in Camus' writings not of radical revisions of metaphysics or later ethical developments (Duff and Marshall 1982: 117), but rather of sobering experiences and excited discoveries as a result of increased consciousness: Caligula and Meursault come to recognize, through their failure to find release in murder, that nihilism is the wrong type of freedom (C, 63); Meursault experiences, within the pressing confines of his prison cell, the way in which an uncompromising negation of any movement away from his condition unlocks in him a profound emotional and spiritual richness and even results in fusion with life as a whole; Sisyphus realizes that acceptance of his fate leads him to happiness beyond hope and endows him with the spirit of revolt, freedom and passion, and the rebel, who starts as a solitary absurd hero, discovers that the reality of the absurd is shared by all others and comes into contact with a "strange form of love" through the sheer power of this understanding (TR, 246).

The absurd, as the healthy acknowledgment of the limits of human existence, also frames limits of behavior and action. While nihilism is the celebration of the wrong freedom, absurdism "does not authorize all actions"; the fact that "everything is permitted does not mean that nothing is forbidden" (MS, 65). Yet the absurd "forbids" not in accordance with some higher ethical system, but as a result of one's own growing awareness of the limits of existence and their organic consequences. Simply put, in the absence of a governing deity, one voluntarily puts limits on oneself. The ending lines of *The Rebel* strongly echo this point: The "men of Europe," impatient with limits, made themselves gods on earth; instead, they ought to "reject the unlimited power" and to "learn to live and to die" – to be a man, they must "refuse to be a god" (TR, 247–248).

In the same way, revolt – one of Camus' "three consequences" – is a human quality and a positive response that springs from a metaphysical reality, that is, from the absurd's fundamental equation. When Duff and Marshall (1982: 128–129) argue that rebellion is "clearly a moral response," which must lean on some self-transcending value, and so Camus' "humanistic ethic of justice, honesty, respect for life, and moderation" should have a more solid foundation, they miss the fact that in *The Myth*, revolt originates from the metaphysical human condition. The impulse to revolt against the limits may not be a "part of the fabric of the universe" (ibid., 124), but it surely constitutes the inherent tension in the fabric of human consciousness.

Camus' eventual sociopolitical humanism grew from absurdism and may be regarded as its expansion to collective dimensions. Scholars seem to favor his post-Second World War statement that, despite the truthfulness of the absurd, "in the end the consequences repel, and I back off from them" (Pölzler 2014: 97). But this "perpetual anxiety" of the "absurd thinker" (ibid., 97), as well as Camus' further philosophical developments, should not lead us to conclude that *The Rebel* created a world upon the ruins of the Sisyphean world. Contrary to expectations, Foley writes (2008: 55), "what is to be found at the beginning of *The Rebel* is a reassertion of the fact of the absurd, as described in *The Myth of Sisyphus.*" Camus is very careful to remain confined to the laws of the universe he himself created and maintains a "continuum in the intellectual trajectory of both essays" (ibid., 56). His declared proposition is to "follow, into the realm of murder and revolt, a mode of thinking that began with suicide and the idea of the absurd" (TR, viii–ix), a task for which he again applies the absurd as a "methodological deconstruction of commonplace assumptions" (Foley 2008: 13). The recognition of the absurd remains a "first necessary step in the development of properly human values" (ibid., 13), as it is a method of negation that makes human consciousness experience life from the inside and thus grow values on a now meaningful earth.

In response to the question of whether the limited and modest absurd universe of *The Myth* could contain *The Rebel*'s seemingly more sophisti-cated, value-based and collective universe, we have Camus' own testimony. "Even as I was writing *The Myth of Sisyphus,*" he explains in an interview, "I was thinking about the essay on revolt that I would write later on" (ibid., 12). *The Rebel* was not a revision of initial premises, but an elaboration on further consequences. Even while toiling over *The Myth*, Camus had not believed that "we could remain at this point" where nothing had a meaning (ibid., 12). Hence, if anything, *The Rebel* exemplifies the dynamics that enable a further evolution of absurdist thought: The positivity of absurdist thought grows from its negative approach while at the same time daring to defy its own conclusions as well as striving to attain an authentically realized life for the absurd human.

Disposing of all tension: Negative responses to the absurd

The responses dismissed by Camus as inadequate actions and modes of living in light of the absurd are all different forms of one impulse: the wish to abolish life's inherent tension and, in doing so, to empty the absurd of its meaning. If one faithfully follows the "commandments of the absurd" (MS, 33) and carries its "logic to its conclusion," one must remain in a state of struggle with a "total absence of hope," but without yielding to despair; "continual rejection," while eschewing renunciation, and "conscious dissatisfaction," which is nothing like "immature unrest" (ibid., 30). Here Camus delineates the uncrossable limit: "Everything that destroys, conjures away, or exercises these requirements" – including sub-missive acceptance – "ruins the absurd" (ibid., 30). Why one should be so careful to keep the absurd alive and intact is less explicitly clear – one may assume that the dynamic tension sustained by absurdity is a constitutive and crucial factor in the development of human consciousness toward its capacity to discover life's internal value; in the absence of tension, the op-portunity to do this would be forever lost.

I shall now briefly explore the responses that Camus believed trans-gress absurd tension.

Suicide and murder

"Must this recognition of 'the walls of absurdity' lead to suicide?" won-ders Smith (2011: 2), but for Camus, there is no starker opposite to the authentic "absurd experience" than suicide (MS, 52). On the face of it, suicide may impress us as an expression of a sober acknowledgment of life's absurdity and its unlivable contradictions; perhaps even as a logical outcome of revolt (ibid., 52), the "ultimate act of human freedom" or the "ultimate act of hubris" (Foley 2008: 10). In reality, it is nothing but "acceptance at its extreme" (MS, 52). The individual who commits suicide "settles the absurd" (ibid., 52), which he only pretends to affirm: Whereas absurd reasoning strives to make life's tensions "the reasons to live," suicide makes them reasons to die (Carroll 2007: 57). In this light, such an act should be understood as a form of nihilism, since "the effects of nihilism are maximized when death seems preferable, or at least as worthy, as continuing" life's struggle (Skrimshire 2006: 288).

This "acceptance at its extreme" greatly differs from Sisyphus' positive response of complete acceptance of one's fate, which constitutes consent to the paradox of life itself: "Living an experience, a particular fate, is accepting it fully" (MS, 51). Ironically, the absurd commands us to live: " 'I experience the feeling of the absurd, therefore I am' – and therefore I will continue to be" (Carroll 2007: 57). In killing oneself, in rushing toward one's "unique and dreadful future" (MS, 52), one ignores the opportunity afforded by life's essential experience as the "man condemned to death" (ibid., 53), one renounces the "possibility of human values," and one gives up on one's only true form of "human freedom" (Foley 2008: 10). The absurd hero, on the other hand, maintains both parts of the absurd's relation by keeping a proper balance between awareness and rejection of death (MS, 52).

The Rebel starts its journey by reaffirming *The Myth*'s "final conclusion" that absurdist reasoning opposes suicide, since it "recognizes human life" – which enables the persistence of the "hopeless encounter" between the questioning human and the universe's silence – as "the single necessary good" (TR, x). This essay's added insight is that absurdism must therefore logically reject any "indifference to life" as the "mark of nihilism" (ibid., x). In this sense, suicide and murder are but "two aspects of a single system": In both cases, it is the mind that refuses limitation and prefers the "dark victory which annihilates earth and heaven" (ibid., xi). Here Camus demonstrates the natural evolution of an ethical response to life, which is really the consequence of an unwavering recognition of the absurd's metaphysical reality.[4]

---

4 Again, it is noteworthy that both Nietzsche and Camus started their line of inquiry by destroying all values and assuming responsibility "for everything alive." Yet Camus criticizes Nietzsche for renouncing the component of rebellion in favor of an

Nihilism

Camus' early works may misguidedly lead some readers to conclude that he is a "defender of nihilism" (Manav 2013: 130). Yet, though he shares the nihilists' "rejection of all value-claims," one must take into account that he considers the act of negation not a doctrine but a method – a "sceptical deconstruction" of all the mental activities that either aim to dissolve the limits of knowledge or powerlessly sink into them (Foley 2008: 7–8). Behind the deconstruction lies a constructive intent: the wish to establish the foundations on which humans could build "a positive ethics" (ibid., 7–8). The emergence of authentic meaning and value could only take place "out of their absence," in "the very nihilistic desert that both negates them and makes them possible" (Carroll 2007: 59).

Indeed, rather than a "prelude to nihilism" (Foley 2008: 7–8), Camus' mission is to transcend nihilism.[5] Perhaps the "first philosopher to examine the absurd as an independent extension of nihilism" (Manav 2013: 126), his absurd heroes exist in the "tension between nihilism and the impulse to resist it" (Skrimshire 2006: 286). Whereas Caligula acknowledges, without relief, that nihilism is the wrong type of freedom, Meursault survives his baptism of fire, realizing that "even within the limits of nihilism it is possible to proceed beyond nihilism" (Foley 2008: 5).

Like suicide, nihilism is not an expression of revolt or a protest against life's absurdity, but rather the final eradication of the metaphysical component of revolt. "Accepting the exigencies dictated by the absurd" should not mean yielding to despair about our creative human capacities (ibid., 56). A letter that Camus wrote to a German friend exemplifies this point well. Camus writes, "You readily accepted despair and I never yielded to it"; in the face of eternal injustice and a universe of unhappiness, "man must exalt justice" and "create happiness" (Duff and Marshall 1982: 125–126).

---

unconditional consent, which, ultimately, "says yes to murder" as well (TR, 44–50). Within the context of this discussion, we can say that Nietzsche did not espouse absurd metaphysics, which necessitates a metaphysical rebellion: the refusal to accept the world as it is.

5 In *The Rebel*, Camus proclaims: "All of us, among the ruins, are preparing a renaissance beyond the limits of nihilism" (TR, 247).

Philosophical suicide

There are "two obvious responses to our frustrations" in the face of a direct encounter with absurd reality: suicide and hope (Aronson 2017: 6–7). Both signify the "mind's retreat before what the mind itself has brought to light" (MS, 48): The first aims to cancel the absurd by eliminating the physical life and the witnessing consciousness that struggles with it; the latter, a remnant of the "religion-inspired effort," is to "imagine and live for a life beyond this life," be it an afterlife or living for some great idea that transcends this life and betrays it by giving it meaning (Aronson 2017: 6–7). Camus sees no essential difference between these two forms of escape, and he therefore refers to hope as "philosophical suicide" (MS, 27). This type of suicide is thought's attempt to find a final release, by means of an idea, from the deadly equation of the absurd. Although it is only natural to "strive to escape the universe of which [one] is the creator" (ibid., 30) and to drown its crushing "uncertainty and contingency" in one's "nostalgia for unity," wishing that absurdity could be circumvented – by recourse to a higher principle or a primordial harmony – implies relieving absurd tension through some "transcendent refuge," thereby ceasing to be a rebel (Smith 2011: 3).

The act of philosophical suicide is broadly tested in *The Myth* in relation to existentialists and phenomenologists, since they are the ones who confronted the absurd, considered it and, eventually, shirked it. To Kierkegaard's impassioned cry – "If the bottomless void that nothing can fill underlay all things, what would life be but despair?" – Camus responds resolutely that "a determined soul will always manage" (MS, 39). He observes two main escape routes in existentialist and phenomenologist thought: either attempting to make the world completely incomprehensible or attempting to make it completely comprehensible (ibid., 47). Both abstract and religious philosophers "start from the same disorder," but one strives for "extreme rationalization" and the other for "extreme irrationalization" (ibid., 46).

"The absurd mind has less luck," writes Camus, since the absurd world is "neither so rational nor so irrational. It is unreasonable" (ibid., 47). Such a mind cannot afford to suppress its nostalgia but is also unable to gather together its universe (ibid., 48). It refuses to make an absolute value out of either hope or despair and allows just enough hope to keep the revolt alive, while avoiding its excesses, which might eventually "minimize the value of this life" (Aronson 2017: 4).

Renunciation

The fifth and last response that aims to terminate absurd tension is the "negation of the world," as pursued in "certain vedantic schools" (MS, 62). Such a total renunciation of human life and human nature – "abandoning one's earthly, individual, human life" for the sake of an identification with the detached "universal viewpoint" – could, indeed, "destroy the other component of the absurd," that is, the experience of the limits of human existence (Nagel 1971: 725–726). Since the absurd can be thought of as the tension between limit and longing, such practices would obviously purge the component of longing as well. Although absurdity might not be annihilated even then – since, as long as one is in human form, one must always "drag the superior awareness" through the "strenuous mundane life" – it would significantly diminish (ibid., 725–726).[6]

Interestingly, Camus does not dismiss this response altogether (nor does Nagel) and even deems it equally as worthy as the positive responses he himself offers.[7] So long as such a path of negation is followed "just as rigorously," one could achieve "similar results," a state somewhat comparable to authentic absurdity as it accomplishes a "veritable 'philosophy of indifference'" (MS, 62). Bowker (2008: 158) writes that for both Grenier, Camus' teacher, and Camus himself, the sage attains a condition of "perfect indifference" and "serene apathy" that frees him or her from everything,

---

6 Or at least one would be less conscious of it, but since "there can be no absurd outside the human mind" (MS, 29), only an outside observer could perceive absurdity in such a person's life.

7 We should be careful not to confuse renunciation with mystical surrender, to which Camus fervently objects. He judges the latter to be a "spiritual leap which basically escapes consciousness": it is a type of freedom that is realized by losing oneself in one's god and, hence, no longer feeling responsible for one's own life (MS, 56–57).

including him- or herself. It is clear, however, that although Camus believes that such a response could potentially liberate one from absurd tension, he does not endorse it, since he is solely interested in retaining that tension.

A true love of life: Positive responses to the absurd

While all negative responses to absurdity boil down to unreadiness to endure the paradox of absurd existence – to make one's "rock" one's "thing" – the positive responses are well founded upon fully conscious consent to human fate, which is now lucidly recognized as the unceasing tension between a rock that is pushed up and a rock that rushes down (MS, 117–118). Indeed, this acceptance is the turning point, the odd miracle that alchemizes the moment of tragic and bitter consciousness of one's "wretched condition" – a moment from which all eluders of absurd reality have pulled back – into a victory (ibid., 117). It is, according to Camus, the one step without which an invaluable opportunity would be missed forever – the possibility of discovering, for oneself, what truly awaits on the other side of absurdity.

I will now briefly introduce Camus' positive responses, particularly the way that acceptance of the absurd establishes the platform upon which an authentically moral relationship with life can naturally emerge.

Acceptance

Acceptance is a choice to embrace the "basic facts of existence" as they have been unveiled through the "dynamic of the immanent conscious process" (Sagi 1994: 283). Would one consciously agree to "take up the heart-rending and marvellous wager of the absurd" (MS, 50)? If philosophical integrity – remaining loyal to one's realization – can be counted as ethics, such a choice would be the second "ethical decision" that one should make, the first being the willingness to face absurdity in the first place (Sagi 1994: 278). Ontologically, Sagi argues (ibid., 283), humans can "either affirm or reject" this "basic datum of their existence," and their ability to do so "attests to their freedom." However, as an "irreducible given" of our experience, the choice is not exactly between affirming or denying it but is rather between responding negatively or positively to it (Carroll 2007: 60). The promise is great: Choosing to live in harmony with this basic datum, "the body, affection, creation, action, human nobility" will all fall into place in "this mad world," and, having united with one's fate, "man will again find there" the wine and bread of indifference on which "he feeds his greatness" (MS, 50–51).

The Sisyphean realization is that "we are our fate, and our frustration is our very life" (Aronson 2017: 8). By becoming conscious of it, and then accepting it, Sisyphus "reshapes his fate into a condition of 'wholly human origin'" (ibid., 9). What strikes us at first as a religious fable – the gods punishing Sisyphus – reveals itself to be a story set in a universe devoid of gods. If there are no gods, there can be no punishment and no resentment either; hence, "a fate is not a punishment" (MS, 72). "What if there are no gods and in a godless world our fate nevertheless does not change?" Carroll wonders (2007: 63), but in true acceptance, the very thought that one could have another fate no longer arises. The reality that the pleasures of the earth must be balanced with an acute awareness of limitations is maturely embraced (Aronson 2017: 9). Thus, a "tremendous remark rings out" in the "wild and limited universe" that "all is well" (MS, 118), and, with this quality of undivided focus, the earth finally becomes "our first and our last love" (TR, 247). In this sense, as in Nietzsche's odyssey of value-making, Camus' first value is the complete affirmation of life.

We must not, however, interpret this acceptance as a "meek submission," since it entails, by nature, a consent to the absurd paradox, which includes both acceptance and "scornful revolt" (Manav 2013: 130). After all, absurdity is an uninterrupted tension, not a relaxation into one's fate, and it feeds on the human resistance to it (ibid., 130). In acceptance, we learn that we cannot help "wishing to go beyond what is possible," and so we agree to "an intensely conscious and active non-resolution" that quickens "our

life-impulses" (Aronson 2017: 9). We accept as much as we resist, even when
it is more a "passive resistance" akin to Sisyphus' joy (Carroll 2007: 65).[8]

Revolt, freedom, passion

Camus' "three consequences" start with revolt, which is, for him, a coherent philosophical – not ethical – position, directly deduced from the
human metaphysical condition: the "constant confrontation between
man and his obscurity" (MS, 52). It is a protest against "the human condition" and "the whole of creation" (TR, 11), as well as "an unlimited cam-
paign against the heavens" (ibid., 13), challenging the world anew every
second through its unreasonable insistence on clarity and unity (MS, 52).
The spirit of revolt maintains the "tension intrinsic to human life" by simultaneously driving one to refuse to accept one's fate and to rebel against
one's mortality and life's limits (Aronson 2017: 7). Thus, revolt counterbalances one's acceptance, in that it eliminates the element of resignation
that accompanies the "certainty of crushing fate," and moreover – since
mere despondent acceptance might render life unworthy of living – it
gives life its value and "restores its majesty" (MS, 52–53). Since the godless
universe fails to live up to our ethical measurement, revolt constitutes a
"mature and creative response" that aims to "contain the destructive potential of the absurd" (Bowker 2008: 171–172) and to "create the justice,
order, and unity" that one sought in vain within one's own condition
(TR, 13). Rather than a destructive force, it is a passionate urge to "re-
create" the universe (Skrimshire 2006: 290); therefore, its attack on the
shattered world is an attempt to "make it whole again" (TR, 11).

The two other consequences – freedom and passion – naturally arise
from the process of negation that has eliminated anything outside the limits
of death, meaning, knowing, and repetition. Since the concept of "freedom"

---

8   Nagel (1971: 727) claims that this response of scornful defiance would be far too dra-
    matic and romantic, given the "cosmic unimportance" of our predicament, and pre-
    scribes instead the approach of "irony." Yet, weeding out revolt – as I previously dem-
    onstrated in relation to Duff and Marshall (1982: 128–129) – brings any discussion of
    Camusean metaphysics to an end.

can no longer be associated with "redemption" or "eternal freedom" – a release from the cosmic prison – it becomes the freedom to be, think and act within the confines of one's cell (MS, 54–55). Paradoxically, the fact that the "only conception of freedom" that has remained is "that of a prisoner" (ibid., 54) relieves the absurd human of his or her anxious anticipation of transcendent liberation; with this profound release from even the subtlest form of waiting, freedom of action is restored and magnified (ibid., 55–57). Hence, the most fundamental freedom is freedom from the future (ibid., 56). What was at first a condemnation is now transformed into liberation, because one is no longer "tied to an eternal vision" (Smith 2011: 3) and should do nothing for the sake of the eternal (MS, 64).

This vision of a "universe without future" (ibid., 89) leads one to exchange the belief in eternal life in the next world with the belief "in eternal life in this world" (ibid., 105), culminating in "unbelievable disinterestedness" toward anything besides the "pure flame of life" (ibid., 58). That is the beginning of a true love of life, life as its own value: refusing "all the 'later on's of this world, in order to lay claim" to one's present wealth – life's riches, which hope has made us neglect, encouraging us instead to gaze out on imagined horizons beyond the limits (Aronson 2017: 4).[9]

Passion is born out of a similar irony: The tragedy of losing all reason and purpose – of having "nothing to live for," no binding "criterion by which things are justified" (Smith 2011: 3) – turns, through the alchemizing power of acceptance, into the ideal of life as the "present and the succession of presents" (MS, 61–62). What cannot be unified becomes multiplied into countless shimmering moments, which are to be lived and thoroughly exhausted (Smith 2011: 3), each time "with the same passion" and with one's "whole self" (MS, 67), since "what counts is not the best living but the most living" (ibid., 60). With the disappearance of one kingdom, there are now, in James Woelfel's words, "many kingdoms of human happiness" that are "rendered all the more precious by their perishability" (Skrimshire 2006: 297). In a world in which experiences never add up

---

9 In Camus' own words from the *Noces*: "The world is beautiful, and outside there is no salvation" (Aronson 2017: 4).

and there is nothing to live for, we live for life. Here again Camus proves
to be a Nietzschean affirmer of the vital forces, a philosopher of life itself.

Human solidarity

How could a process that started with a "denial of value" end in a "philosophy of action" (Smith 2011: 3)? At this point, that should no longer
puzzle us. It is already clear how an unreserved negation leads to complete
consciousness of absurd reality, which, in turn, gives rise to acceptance as
an inevitable philosophical lucidity. Acceptance leads to an absurd form
of unification with human fate; as one's "passionate attention" remains
undivided in its focus on the only life one has (MS, 57), resolving to draw
one's strength from the universe such as it is (ibid., 58), the spirit of revolt,
freedom and passion gives birth to a love of life, which embraces and validates life as the "single necessary good" (TR, x). Thus far, this could be
fairly equated with Nietzsche's "amor fati." From this point, at which life
becomes its own value and the universe can be experienced only from
the inside, the so-called ethical leap to human solidarity is short: Having
achieved his unique happiness, Sisyphus' awareness continues to grow,
enough to look around, and away from his "solipsistic exile," to discover
the many brothers and sisters who share the very same fate under the blistering sun of absurdity (Foley 2008: 58). This recognition enables him to
expand his newfound love of life to a love of all that lives (ibid., 56).

The immense form of active empathy, demonstrated by Camus in *The
Rebel*, emanates from both acceptance and revolt. Acceptance, through
its unequivocal rejection of suicide and nihilism, as well as philosophical
suicide and renunciation, blesses life as the only necessary good, a blessing
that extends to all humans (TR, x), who are "overwhelmed by the same
strangeness of things" and by the same division and unhappiness, and
who similarly seek to come to terms with their agonizing fate (ibid., 10).
This organic realization – that the absurd condition is the human condition – "permits an important reorientation of the absurd premise" (Foley
2008: 57). As Camus put it in a 1945 interview, "Why not admit that a

mind which is pessimistic about the human condition can still feel within himself a solidarity with his companions in servitude?" (ibid., 4).[10]

Such a feeling is the beginning of absurd compassion, a "strange form of love" that is non-religious by nature and yet echoes saintly sentiments when it cries: "If all are not saved, what good is the salvation of one only?" (TR, 246). Now, the evolved absurd hero "identifies himself with humanity in general" (ibid., 4) and, through this identification, realizes that we, who are fated to live side by side in this silent world, should "seek to build a new home" upon this earth, which will "replace external or metaphysical reality" (Sagi 2002: 23), limiting our concerns to "what is before us" rather than investing in some unreal future of universal human happiness (Duff and Marshall 1982: 131).

The metaphysical component of revolt lends an element of active insurgence to this new type of human solidarity. The awakening of the absurd hero to collective unhappiness and universal compassion transforms the revolt from an individual protest against an indifferent universe into a shared rebellion against both cosmic and human injustice, since arbitrariness and unreasonableness exist to the same degree in the man-made world. We are "crushed between human evil and destiny, between terror and the arbitrary" (TR, 246). As both absurd individuals and a society, our revolt should also be directed toward resistance to the potential destructive forces inherent in an illogical misinterpretation of our absurd nature that might cause it to degenerate into a perverted form of unbridled nihilism (Foley 2008: 4).

10 Camus' 1956 novel, *The Fall*, echoes these sentiments of absurdist solidarity. Its protagonist, Jean-Baptiste Clamence, poetically declares: "Covered with ashes, tearing my hair, my face scored by clawing, but with piercing eyes, I stand before all humanity recapitulating my shames without losing sight of the effect I am producing and saying: 'I was the lowest of the low.' Then imperceptibly I pass from the 'I' to the 'we.' When I get to 'This is what we are,' the game is over and I can tell them off. I am like them, to be sure; we are in the soup together" (Camus 2000: 103). And to a woman whose suicide he witnessed, he imagines himself saying: "O young woman, throw yourself into the water again so that I may a second time have the chance of saving both of us! A second time, eh, what a risky suggestion! Just suppose, cher maître, that we should be taken literally? We'd have to go through with it. Brr ...! The water's so cold!" (ibid., 107–108).

In *The Rebel* (224–227), Camus carefully delineates the misguided logic of moral nihilism, proving that it is by nature a denial of the absurd condition. Conceptualizing what he demonstrated in the narratives of *The Stranger* and *Caligula*, he contends that nihilism falsely assumes total freedom, rejects any limit, and interprets the fact that we all share the destiny of the man condemned to death as permission to kill. The absurd rebel, however, perceives social injustice as a continuation of universal injustice and therefore resists both. This constitutes the birth of a different logic: The realization that freedom must be relative and limited, since the freedom one claims for oneself should be claimed for all. Furthermore, in light of the fact that rebellion is a "protest against death," it cannot logically end in any destructive form of rebellion, but only in claiming the unity of the human condition and serving it as a force of life and creation.

At the same time, rebellion must take the form of an unyielding opposition to grand "political and religious ideas and ideologies," in the attempt to preserve the "greatest value of all" (Carroll 2007: 66) – what Camus finally terms "human nature" (TR, 4). Since the rebel "disclaims divinity" to share in the "destiny of all men" (TR, 248) – while driving out of this world a god who calls on us to give up any concern for it (Skrimshire 2006: 294–295) – we assume full responsibility for a planet that is now solely ours. For when we know that "this prison cell" is "all we have and all we need," rebellion becomes a form of social transformation too (ibid., 297, 289).

Are Camus' three responses – acceptance, the spirit of revolt, freedom and passion, and human solidarity – sufficiently effective in the way they handle the suffocating experience of limits in human existence? To some extent, they are. Complete acceptance does allow a unification of mind and fate, evoking authentic peace and joy in the human heart. The "consequences" enable a harmonious and creative co-existence with the limits and the capacity to redefine freedom and passion within their boundaries, largely owing to the fact that Camus' metaphysics permits defiance against the limits while maintaining them as one's unchanging reality. Whereas acceptance alone would have dissipated life's flame in us, revolt counterbalances this acceptance with the dynamism of human spirit. Lastly, human solidarity makes it possible to dissolve some of the ingrained universal strangeness. Even if the universe forever remains a stranger to us, at least mortal beings can find closeness through the recognition of a shared destiny.

To this array of human responses, we should add the act of art as a positive response to absurdity. In *The Rebel*, Camus dedicates many pages to the argument that art should be seen as a direct expression of the metaphysical component of rebellion. For him, art is the insistence on attaining impossible unity and the rejection of the world as it is. Art snatches from history's grasp the project of a future absolute beauty and fabricates its own substitute universe, in which it can reign and attain total justice. Nonetheless, the intention of this competition with God's world is not to escape reality, but truly to transcend it, only to eventually "make this mortal and limited world ... more appealing than any other" (TR, 198–203). The make-believe history of the novel, for instance, is "a rectification of the world we live in" (TR, 207), an attempt to reduce our sense of strangeness in it. Such an approach may also validate the project of science fiction film as a maker of substitute futures whose intention is not to promote the escapist spirit, but rather to defy our current, limited worldview in a way that can correct our vision of the possibilities of this life and this universe.

Now that Camus' range of human responses to absurdity is spread before us, it is time to place the universe of this humanist French philosopher next to the imagined universes of the four science fiction films I have chosen. Will an analysis of their philosophical and symbolical contents echo the limits of human experience, as presented in Chapter 2, or, alternatively, call them into question and throw new light on them? And will such a reading resonate with the scope of negative and positive responses to the absurd condition, as outlined in this chapter, or challenge them, perhaps even offering further responses overlooked by Camus' works?

PART II

Science fiction films: Absurd at the edge of the cosmos

In Chapters 4 and 5, I will bring four science fiction films into dialogue with Camus' philosophy of the absurd. My hypothesis – that such an interaction could be instigated at all – is grounded in the growing field of philosophy of science fiction film, which perceives films of this genre as philosophical exercises that center on the nature of human consciousness and existence (Sanders 2008: 1, 26–27). In particular, the way these films viscerally portray the meeting point and collision between humans and nonhumans could be thought of as an unintentional methodology: "confronting this otherness" – that which is only superficially different from us – is like "having a mirror held up in front of our faces" (Rowlands 2005: viii). It is not unreasonable to deduce from this that, as an integral part of their role as thought-experiments that assess the boundaries and limits of our existence, they should also include an exploration into the absurd component of the human condition. I will therefore seek to bring into conversation what at first may appear to be disparate streams of thought: Camus' purely humanistic philosophy, and films that imagine traveling far beyond the human perspective in a seemingly escapist spirit. By incorporating the two in one line of inquiry, one should be able to shed more light on their somewhat similar interest in studying the limits of human experience, as revealed through humans' relationship with the cosmos, and one's authentic chances of finding meaning and redemption within those limits. This will allow me to take an as yet unexplored direction, that of extrapolating what might happen when the absurd hero takes leave of planet Earth and its familiar conditions.

Although none of these films refers directly or consciously to Camus' absurd,[1] I shall consider certain aspects of their thought-experiments in the light of the absurd. The task is easy, since all four films are packed with visions and dialogues that echo Camusean metaphysics, as well as the variety of responses to absurd awakening that Camus closely scrutinized. Since science fiction widens the landscape in which the human search unfolds to cosmic measures, the Sisyphean universe becomes even more oppressive, and the longing to find one's place in an estranging world more acute. All five limits – separation, knowing, meaning, death, and repetition – appear to confine both mankind and the alien or A.I. "species" that compete with human beings in the absurd prison, from which they ponder possible means of escape. The films' characters, nonhuman and human alike, struggle with the punishment inflicted by the gods in ways that range from Camus' negative responses – murder, suicide, philosophical suicide, and renunciation – to the positive, such as acceptance, revolt, freedom, and passion. Human, and even intergalactic, solidarity and love emerge, from both sides, as ways of overcoming meaninglessness and cosmic emptiness.

This brings us to the question of the relevance of Camus' absurd to the philosophy of science fiction film. I would suggest that it is a generally constructive perspective that illumines many unexplored aspects of the narratives. Not only is absurdity sustained as a verifiable description of existence in the universe, but, in an unforced manner, it provides the films with an undeniable layer of insight. It is therefore surprising that Camus' philosophy is a neglected perspective in sci-fi film philosophy, and, more generally, in film philosophy.

Undoubtedly, a superficial reading of the films enables the Camus scholar to instantly detect such absurdist components. Yet a deeper probing into their metaphorical webs, underlying themes and narrative resolutions, which strives to gather their philosophical content into coherent statements about the human condition, further reveals how they either "reject" or "expand" those components. In this sense, the

---

1   Moreover, I have not found evidence indicating that any of the makers of these films – screenwriters or directors – have viewed their works in light of absurdism.

Camus–sci-fi dialogue involves a kind of mutually informing critical comparison: Certain aspects of the films are brought more sharply into view when they are analyzed in the light of the absurd, and Camus' absurd is illuminated – and some of its limitations are exposed – when it is brought into dialogue with sci-fi films.

This critical comparison enables me to read the films as provoking re-evaluations of the viability of Camus' philosophy under extremely different conditions. I will do this following two major lines of inquiry. The first will be to question whether the films contradict, confirm, or expand the Camusean description of the relation between human beings and the universe they inhabit. Would the absurd predicament be any different in an altogether unfamiliar universe or in the future, thus undermining the resilience of Camus' philosophy? Could absurd nature be viewed in a different light, calling for other responses to it? The second layer of inquiry will be the following: Suppose we finally got to know aliens, or alternatively managed to create highly advanced robots – species that similarly and undeniably possessed self-reflective minds – would they, despite the different conditions of their existence, experience the absurd in the same way and to the same extent? And, following from that, might we discover that the human experience of absurdity is unique? Obviously, whatever form or absence of the absurd that we may ascribe to other beings is no more than a projection. Paraphrasing Nagel's (1974) words, we are not capable of establishing what it is like to be an alien or a robot, and so it is not possible for us to comprehend any condition other than the human condition. However, it is exactly this that has been the source of my curiosity – whatever we project onto such holograms of the future tells us much about us humans of the present.

I could easily think of a long list of sci-fi films the interpretation of which would greatly benefit from the application of a conceptual lens informed by Camus' notion of the absurd, as well as further supporting or questioning the consistency of my own findings, for example, *2001: A Space Odyssey* (1968), *Solaris* (1972), *Blade Runner* (1982), *The Abyss* (1989), *Dark City* (1998), *District 9* (2009), *Knowing* (2009), *Moon* (2009), *Never Let Me Go* (2010), *Prometheus* (2012), *Gravity* (2013), *Interstellar* (2014), and

Ex-Machina (2014).[2] The four selected films, though fairly well known among cineastes and film-philosophers and critically acclaimed, may not be the typical selection for Camus' first contact with the sci-fi genre. One may question these choices, in light of the fact that no major science fiction film has been analyzed in connection with Camus' theme of the absurd as of yet. Just think of *2001*'s featureless alien monolith that consistently catapults humanity into evolutionary leaps while forever remaining incomprehensible, thus only emphasizing human longing and loneliness. Or recall *Solaris'* conscious planet that gives "no answers, only choices" as it entraps its human visitors in an eternal repetition of their past. We could go as far as to argue that the absence of any genuine partner on the other side of these cosmic dialogues enhances the absurdity even more. Against this conventional expectation, I would suggest that these somewhat offbeat pathways can help in showing how the genre can be stretched to cover new territory. The two following chapters are, nevertheless, more an invitation to further study: one that would, among others, satisfy the need for elaborate absurdist interpretations of the more classic works of the genre.

---

2   A different set of films, bearing a scholarly attractiveness of its own, would be science fiction films that were made and screened during the time in which Camus developed his absurdist thought. Was he aware of the rise of the genre during the 1950's? Did he notice landmark sci-fi films such as *The Thing from Another World* (1951), *The Day the Earth Stood Still* (1951), *Forbidden Planet* (1956), and *Invasion of the Body Snatchers* (1956)?

CHAPTER 4

When the silent universe speaks: Applying Camus' absurd to the alien encounters of *Contact* and *Arrival*

Both Robert Zemeckis' *Contact* (1997) and Denis Villeneuve's *Arrival* (2016) vividly announce in their opening scenes their intention to explore a tension, as well as a potential meeting point, between the ordinary human condition and a vaster cosmic, or at least beyond-human, consciousness.

Contact's opening shot begins with a view of earth from outer space, still close enough to detect its hubbub of contemporary radio and television chatter and sound. But the camera swiftly pulls back from the blue planet and retreats into deep space, gradually disengaging from the human drama. As the camera passes other planets in our solar system, the radio and television music and news reports rapidly go back in time to their earliest broadcast at the beginning of twentieth century. What, on earth, have been considered major historical turning points – human triumphs and atrocities alike – subside as the camera pulls back even further, out of the Milky Way and the cluster of galaxies of which it is part. This vision is reminiscent of the thought-experiment – the Pale Blue Dot – suggested by astronomer Carl Sagan (1994),[1] who challenged us to radically question "our imagined self-importance" in light of the humbling cosmological reality of our planet as a "lonely speck in the great enveloping cosmic dark." Now, swallowed by numerous galaxies, nebulae and the immensity of space, silence prevails, making the entire human experience, with all its breakthroughs and limitations, seem like an odd, distant dream. The human cry is subdued by the astounding, but empty beauty of Camus' silent and indifferent universe.

---

1 It is no coincidence that Sagan had authored the novel *Contact*, which he toiled to bring to the screen during the final seventeen years of his life; sadly, he died while the film was being filmed (Svetkey, 1997).

But just when the "silence, relentless movement, and the sheer size of the space" start to "become oppressive," the camera concludes its cosmic journey by emerging from the eye of a young girl (Krämer 2013: 128). This shot, which moves from the earthly stage to the vast cosmic arena, finally reveals itself as one that is contained within an individual mind, thus establishing a unity of inner and outer, human and universe. Our distinction between the subjective and the objective is momentarily shaken, but we soon return to the familiar absurd duality of a silent universe and human longing: We find the child leaning against her CB radio, imploring the universe to finally speak. Here the film communicates its central theme, which coincides with Camus' metaphysics: "Man's unconscious feelings in the face of his universe: an insistence upon familiarity" (MS, 15).

Arrival also begins by juxtaposing human experience with a transhuman perspective.[2] We hear a woman's voice-over, which is contrasted by the onscreen image of large windows framed by a dark, enclosing space: "I used to think this was the beginning of your story. Memory is a strange thing. It doesn't work like I thought it did. We are so bound by time, by its order." As this last sentence is spoken, we are presented with a series of vignettes, which exemplify this time-bound order: a mother accompanying her child from birth to childhood to adolescence to premature death. That is the human chronology to which we are bound; the unstoppable pattern of the "man condemned to death" (MS, 53). However, the images of the girl's life subtly prepare the viewer for a shift in perception. Her birth and death mirror one another: First, the newborn lies motionless in bed and the mother's expression could be interpreted as an expression of grief, and later, in an identical position, the adolescent's still body lies in a hospital's bed; the new mother takes her crying baby from unknown hands, lovingly saying "Come back to me," and then sobs next to her daughter's corpse, saying the very same words.

Through this sense of a beginning that is also an end, and a life that consumes itself before it begins, the voice-over makes us conscious of the shift in perspective: "But now I'm not sure I believe in beginnings and

---

2 I use "transhuman" in its literal sense, and not as it has been employed by the transhumanist movement.

endings. There are days that define your story beyond your life. Like the day they arrived." These ironic opening lines further undermine the relation between the screen image and its verbal description, affording us what Nagel (1986) called "the view from nowhere": a transcendent view, unbound by time and its order, that invades ordinary perception and separates consciousness from human experience. A moment later, linguist Dr. Louise Banks appears before her students, describing language as "an expression of art" – that is, language can depart from any linear obligation and reshuffle life's sequence as it pleases.

The underlying thematic similarity of *Contact* and *Arrival* extends far beyond their opening scenes. In both films, the silent universe suddenly begins to speak in a language that humans struggle to comprehend. In *Contact*, a transmission from the star Vega reaches Dr. Eleanor Arroway, a SETI (Search for Extraterrestrial Intelligence) project scientist, as if in response to her childhood plea; what seems at first to be an audio signal reveals a hidden video and 63,000 pages of indecipherable data. In *Arrival*, twelve 1,500-foot, elongated, oval-shaped spacecraft appear out of the blue at different, inexplicably connected locations on earth. The faceless aliens that inhabit them, humanly called "Heptapods" because of their seven limbs, seem to express themselves emotionally through incomprehensible groans and vibrations, but they slowly disclose their second, more intellectual language, a stunningly otherworldly visual language, which they are eager to teach humans.[3] Much of the plot of each film is dedicated to the earthlings' efforts to comprehend and respond to the aliens' transmissions, their failures to do so and the way in which their collision with the alien language reflects the limits of human experience.[4] In both films, the earnest attempts of the heroines to decipher and answer the messages lead them to

3 The complex calligraphy, which is organically produced by an ink emitted from the Heptapods' bodies, consists of individual, circular logograms, thus expressing a perception that has no beginning and no end.

4 *Arrival*'s director, Denis Villeneuve, said in an interview that the film is all about the "tension of a cultural exchange" and that is why it "takes the time to explore the limits of language," in order to lead to the insight that "the only way to communicate is through intuition" (Thompson, 2017). This, as we shall see, can be easily applied to *Contact* as well.

temporarily merge their minds with the alien minds, as a direct outcome of which they have transcendent, cosmic experiences during which they perceive as the aliens perceive. Finally, the two plots deal with the lasting impact of the cosmic event on Harroway's and Banks' experiences of their limited human existence.

The thematic commonalities of the two films strike me as a promising foundation for a unified exploration of absurdity. I shall therefore set my analyses of the films side by side, deliberately focusing on their connecting threads rather than their dissimilarities. I will start with the shared characteristics of the two heroines.

The struggle for unity

After their intentionally disorienting opening scenes, the two films introduce us to the main characters. *Contact* presents us with astronomer Dr. Eleanor "Ellie" Arroway, and *Arrival* with linguist Dr. Louise Banks. Both are female scientists who are soon destined to take on the task of deciphering a seemingly incomprehensible, unworldly language. But what makes them more capable than others of decoding transmissions of a higher, transcendent order?

Interestingly, Ellie and Louise alike are portrayed as strangers in their own world, intensely detached, impersonal and excessively dedicated to their work. In *Contact*, a short scene from Ellie's childhood provides important clues regarding the origins of her later detachment. Ellie, the same child in whose consciousness the entire cosmic journey unfolded, leans against her CB radio, pleading for contact. Having had some success in reaching Pensacola, Florida, she asks her father whether they could, in like manner, talk to the moon and to Jupiter; soon after, she poignantly wonders: "Could we talk to Mom?" His response compels Ellie to come up against Camus' uncrossable limit of death: "I don't think even the biggest radio could reach that far." One could perhaps contact Jupiter, but one could never look beyond death's barriers. This scene makes it clear that Ellie's appetite for science is indistinguishably intermixed with a private hope, a combination that results in a profound "nostalgia for unity" (MS, 48), that is, the restoration of a once lost sense of connectedness. This recalls Bowker's (2008: 156) suggestion that when natural union fails, metaphysical thought seeks to compensate and to offer a union of its own by striving to make the universe known and familiar. Since Ellie wants to know if there are "people on other planets" shortly after hearing that she could never reach her Mom, it is reasonable to conclude that much of her zeal for communicating with the impossible – after all, even alien life forms are more reachable than the dead – is a transformation of her original, more emotional longing for reunion (Ebert, 1997). This is indicated by the way in which the shot of the little girl sitting by her radio at nighttime, deciding that she would need a bigger antenna, dissolves into a shot of the adult Ellie looking at a huge radio telescope. This magical wish-fulfillment establishes the film's story as the "externalization of the protagonist's subjectivity" (Krämer 2013: 132).

One sentence that is repeated three times in *Contact* – "If it is just us, it seems like an awful waste of space" – establishes the film's main theme, that of private and cosmic loneliness. The nothingness into which her mother has vanished (and later her father too, ironically while Ellie is occupied observing through her telescope) is, in the film's vision, the same impenetrable sterile infinity that surrounds humanity's absurdly isolated culture. Space, in which she hopes to discover life, is equated with death and so raising one's head toward the heavens is akin to seeking to find the afterworld.[5] When we encounter Ellie as an adult, she is a disillusioned orphan, blind to the human world around her, who avoids opportunities for earthly intimacy and devotes her entire emotional longing to a possible union with the heavens. Camus could easily blame her, and possibly Sagan as well, for wishing to commit "philosophical suicide" – the hope to be rescued from the limits of human experience by some external force while

---

5 Alfonso Cuarón's *Gravity* (2013) is another significant film that features at its center a grieving woman who floats in deep space, which symbolizes death and emptiness, but also an opportunity for a new life. Similarly to *Contact*, after she comes to terms with the loss of her daughter, she is once again free to fully return to earth.

overlooking the only life we have.[6] Indeed, the film itself critically reflects her unwillingness to realize earthly contacts.

Louise Banks, *Arrival*'s heroine, appears to be a highly disconnected and indifferent person. This is partly because of the film's manipulation of the sequence of events: its explicit intention to foster in the viewer the misconception that Louise's daughter lived and died before its story commences. Hence, the viewer wrongly interprets Louise's odd behavior as a grieving process that has not come to a close and naturally assumes that her remoteness originates from the same sense of unbearable loss, as in *Contact*. Its visual style is characterized by enclosing, extreme darkness, which creates an unnerving, intimate and somber mood (Carruthers 2018: 324), Louise paces through the university's halls and corridors, bizarrely incurious about the fact that nearly all students have gathered around the windows and only a handful have chosen to attend her lecture. She tries to ignore the constant ringing of her students' mobile phones, until finally forced by one student to turn the TV to a news channel, whereupon she witnesses for the first time the historical report of the landing of the twelve alien objects. Even then, in the midst of chaos and hysteria, she remains a distant observer, unable to take part in her mother's anxiety, saying blankly of her own emotional state that she is "about the same"; a day later, she insists on returning, as usual, to an utterly empty university and lecture hall. As a linguist who cannot speak and a profoundly dissociated woman, she herself seems like an alien, her home like a spaceship, floating in isolation from events and people.

This alienness, however, somehow endows both Ellie and Louise with a unique capacity to keep their ears open to nonhuman transmissions. They may not be able to speak "human" that well, but they exhibit impressive skillfulness when it comes to speaking "cosmic" and bridging the two languages. They approach the aliens in an unmediated, personal way, and they are chosen by the aliens for exactly that reason. Although both are scientists, they allow the feminine and the intimate to guide them. Indeed,

6 Bohlin (1998) criticizes Sagan for considering aliens a non-religious messiah that could save us from ourselves. Yet this does not seem to be unique to Sagan: *Arrival*, as we will see, repeats the very same principle.

the hidden message of both films is that only the emotional, intuitive connection can overcome what Camus considered the limit of separation.[7]

In *Contact*, Ellie is clearly not a conventional scientist, though she certainly makes a concerted effort to seem like one. Sagan's widow, Ann Druyan, who wrote the film's story outline with him, explained in an interview that "we wanted to do a story about a woman like Carl," which to them implied "a character driven in an almost Old Testament way by the need to know the truth" (Svetkey, 1997). This tireless drive of a Biblical prophet is, in Ellie, an amalgam of emotional pain and its mutation into science, a vehemently denied spiritual longing for union, and a genuine scientific passion. As a result of these components, her listening to the cosmos is urgent and acute; her wish is less for scientific discovery and more for actual contact that would be strong enough to dissipate cosmic loneliness. In one shot, just before the dramatic moment when the alien signal is received, we see several huge radio antennas lined up in a way that is reminiscent of the known monolithic human figures on Easter Island: those giant-headed statues that raise their faces with anticipation toward the sky. As the camera tilts down, Ellie is revealed, in the very same position. She has become an antenna herself, her whole being positioned to receive.

Since Ellie's character is designed to struggle to cover up the origins of her attraction to the alien encounter, she is surrounded by two characters who mirror those emotional and spiritual aspects of herself until she is able to consciously embrace them. The first is Kent, her blind colleague, whose impairment makes it possible for him to engage more intimately with the universal transmissions, as if from within. The second is Palmer Joss, a young theologian, author, and a presidential spiritual counselor.

---

7 By associating "feminine" with "intimate," "emotional," and "intuitive," I do not convey my own worldview, but that of the films: indeed, the two films seem to both challenge and endorse traditional feminine stereotypes. As talented female scientists who confidently steer their colleagues toward breakthroughs, they defy stereotypical expectations, yet what endows them with such capacities – and distinguishes them from the war-hungry, over-rational and secretly fearful men that surround them – is their feminine sensibilities. This is even more complex as Ellie is presented as being torn between her hard-nosed approach to knowledge and her intuition, which eventually wins.

Palmer represents Ellie's unconscious emotional and spiritual quest. He is motivated by a life-changing spiritual experience, which echoes Ellie's own scientific endeavor: While he was "looking at the sky," all of a sudden he became filled with the feeling that he was not alone. Palmer responds to her suggestion that he may have had this experience because some part of him needed to have it by insisting on inner knowing as an unverifiable transcendent recognition, stating that, "My intellect couldn't even touch this." In this, he is like a Chestov or a Kierkegaard, both criticized by Camus for violating the limit of knowing through their "sacrifice of the intellect" (MS, 36). Palmer keeps pointing out that the real issue is the deep-seated and much overlooked hunger of the human heart; the fact that despite scientific advances, "we feel emptier and more cut off from each other," devoid of any sense of direction. His symbol of what really matters is a toy compass, which he hands Ellie, hinting that emotional connection and the spiritual longing for union are the keys to navigating an incomprehensible universe, as well as the depths of one's own incomprehensible self. Palmer's stance corresponds well with Camus' advancement of human solidarity as a proper response to the absurd: The answer to cosmic loneliness is one another.

Despite her character's need for external representations of her irrational and intuitive drives, Ellie's reaction to the signals from Vega is explicitly distinguished from the reactions of her fellow scientists, government officials, and the public. She seems to trust the aliens' intention almost religiously, strongly resisting the masculine, militaristic and oppressive elements that invade her intimate space of listening. She remains steadfast, even when the signal's first layer is decoded, revealing no less than a video of Hitler initiating the Olympics in 1936, which further incites the war-like spirit, suspicion, paranoia and fragmentation around her. When the message is finally decrypted as the schematics for a complex machine that is determined to be a sort of a transport for a single traveler, she is willing to blindly follow the aliens' manual, even though the odd spacecraft lacks a chair, a restraining harness, survival gear and recording equipment. Significantly, in Sagan's novel, the transport is meant for five occupants – the film's choice to dramatically turn it into a one-seat spacecraft proposes to view the cosmic journey as a journey into one's own consciousness, in which the universe is as subjective as it is objective. We are left to wonder whether it is Ellie's overwhelming desire for unity that spurs on the silent cosmos to finally speak.

In *Arrival*, the heroine Louise, who is indifferent to the human world around her, reveals profound emotional capacities for trust and intimacy and a passion for direct communication as soon as she is introduced to the opportunity of contact with the aliens. As a linguist, she considers language to be the "glue that holds people together," the power that can either encourage separation or lead to unity. Louise is contrasted with Ian, a theoretical physicist who believes in the superiority of science as a universal language, unlike *Contact*'s Palmer. He is muscularly eager to elicit scientific knowledge from the aliens, but she stops him and asks, "How about we just talk to them before we start throwing math problems at them?" Unlike all the other emissaries who have been selected to enter into dialogue with the aliens, for Louise the glass wall that stands between them quickly turns from an untraversable limit of separation into a transparent meeting point, where the two can become one in mind.[8] In Ted Chiang's *The Story of Your Life* (2016: 5), the novella that inspired *Arrival*, this movement toward union is well captured: "The looking glass appeared to grow transparent; it was as if someone was slowly raising the illumination behind tinted glass. The illusion of depth was uncanny; I felt I could walk right into it."[9] Louise takes brave steps toward this limit – which is like the imagined distance between the universe and oneself – and insists on personalizing the encounter, making it individual in a humanly familiar way. To everyone's shock, she removes her protective gear, saying "They need to see me," presses her hand against the glass wall, and names the two aliens. Like Ellie, she is carried away by the longing to lift the veil between

---

8 This transparent glass wall, encompassed by edgeless darkness, is only one example of the way in which the camera generally frames people, objects and aliens, symbolizing a transcendental window to infinity. Fleming and Brown (2018: 342) describe this as a "dark contact lens," which allows us to see "that which to humans is typically in darkness," drawing perception "towards the future and the cosmic."

9 There may be an implicit allusion here to Lewis Carroll's *Through the Looking-Glass*: Like Alice, Louise climbs through a mirror into a world that she can see beyond it only to find that – as in a reflection – everything, including logic, is reversed in that other world (M. Burley 2019, personal communication, 16 April).

herself and the mysteries of the universe, willing to take the deadly risk of removing all defenses. To begin to speak its language, whose grammar is "perfectly ambiguous" (Chiang 2016: 30), we ought to "lend ourselves to its life," understand it through our body, and let it inhabit our being to the point that we "cannot tell what comes from me and what from it" (Richard 2018: 42, 44).

While Louise's exceptional longing is rewarded by the universe's agents – they switch from their vocal language to their visual language and even press one of their appendages against the glass to craft with her a circular logogram in a unified flow – her growing intimacy with them is contrasted with intense governmental, militaristic and public paranoia. As in *Contact*, this contrast enables us to identify the heroine as an ideal candidate for the cosmic encounter. The same language that draws Louise toward communion is interpreted by everyone else in the spirit of separation. As Bowker (2008: 141) shows, Camus' limit of separation may indicate not a resisting universe, but rather an ambivalence within human consciousness regarding unity and individuality. Terms used in the aliens' visual language, such as "Use weapon" (which really means "Tools") or "The many become one" (which is intended to encourage planetary oneness), only elicit people's dread of extermination. Since the aliens in both *Contact* and *Arrival* are, in a sense, but a looking glass through which humanity's own self-destructive forces are reflected, we can say that the language with which we approach the universe – be it separative or unitive – is exactly what is thrown back at us.

Now that we have examined the human aspect, let us turn to the common design of extraterrestrials in *Contact* and *Arrival*.

The gods of the universe

In both films, the aliens serve a dual role. Their first role is as complex life forms who are similar to humans in that they too possess a self-reflective mind, though theirs is clearly far superior to humans' in its cognitive functions and scientific insight. As previously shown in Chapter 2, from Camus' point of view, the very experience of having a mind that stands out from creation is absurdity itself, since it necessitates a split between life and the consciousness of life, which makes the longing for unity innate as well as inevitable. This fundamental condition subjects the aliens to the laws of the absurd universe, and implies that, in opposition to Camus' definition of absurdity as an exclusively human predicament, enduring the absurd is the mark of self-reflective consciousness in whatever form it may take. Symptoms of this paradoxical existence within a universe that will not betray its meaning can be easily identified in *Contact*'s and *Arrival*'s extraterrestrials, even though the limits their minds must come up against are not as tight or as suffocating.

In *Contact*, when Ellie is pushed to convey to Palmer her personal motivation for embarking on such a life-endangering journey to Vega, she says: "For as long as I can remember, I've been searching for ... some reason why we're here. What are we doing here? Who are we?" This statement discloses an expectation that the aliens would assume the role of the mystical God and would be able to relieve her and humanity as a whole of its limits of knowing and meaning. Yet, after she is taken on an awe-inspiring cosmic voyage within the alien spacecraft and both her and the viewer's expectations reach a peak, the encounter itself, despite being emotionally satisfying, is rather disappointing, since the alien, embodied as her deceased father, has absolutely no meaningful answer and is almost as confused as she is. In response to Ellie's question, "Why did you contact us?" he answers, "You contacted us. We were just listening" – which means that both sides were merely reflecting each other's longing for communion. His ultimate conclusion about the meaning of life is also frustrating: "In all our searching, the only thing we've found that makes the emptiness bearable is each other."[10] He has no idea how the transport system came into being in the first place, so it seems that its only role is to initiate the creation of bonds

10 This is compatible not only with Camus' limit of meaning and his positive response of human solidarity, but also with Palmer's view that associates humanity's crisis of meaning with the loss of its ability to connect and relate. As soon as Ellie receives from the alien the same answer to her heart's deeper yearning, thus confirming Palmer's view, *Contact* closes the earth–heaven circle and establishes its message.

and to supply all isolated cultures with a reassuring sense of togetherness within a terrifyingly senseless universe. It is only through this emotional connectedness that self-reflective minds can overcome the cosmic emptiness. Hence, the absurd cannot be overcome through the aliens' greater cognitive functions or phenomenal scientific advancement, since these cannot break the limit of meaning that stubbornly safeguards the "why" of all existence. As Bryan (2016: 4) puts it, "Twenty-six light years and all we get is a cure for interplanetary angst!"

Arrival's aliens are also entrapped in a peculiar absurd condition: Endowed with a simultaneous, rather than sequential, mode of awareness, which allows them to transcend linear order and to experience "all events at once" (Chiang 2016: 30–31), they are consciously bound to a fate that they are unable to change. For instance, they participate enthusiastically in a conversation though they are already familiar with its eventual outcome (ibid., 33), because they must actualize the conversation "for their knowledge to be true" (ibid., 34). Thus, for them, any humanly spontaneous discourse is a mere "ritual recitation" (ibid., 35). Even though Chiang's novella carefully explicates their state of consciousness as a paradoxical one, which far surpasses rigid human concepts of either free will or determinism (ibid., 33), one cannot deny its absurdist aspect, which further tightens Camus' limit of repetition: Merely enacting one's foreseen chronology seems to intensify the sense that we "continue making the gestures commanded by existence" (MS, 4) and the awkward feeling that, in a universe in which "nothing is possible but everything is given" (ibid., 58), "there is no future" (ibid., 56). In light of the aliens' obligation to powerlessly yet wholeheartedly engage in the drama of their life, Nagel's (1971: 725) comment that the absurd condition only comes into play when a transcendent consciousness is involved – causing us to lead a "meagre yet frantic life" without being able to rise above our own programming – becomes even more acutely relevant. In Chiang's story, the Heptapods arrive and leave for no apparent reason (Chiang 2016: 38), whereas in *Arrival*, the alien explains to Louise that they have come to help humanity because "in 3,000 years we will need humanity's help." This explanation, however, only aggravates the absurd circularity of their condition: Even their apparent intervention is predetermined.

Yet, as well as actively participating in the absurd condition, both alien life forms play a second role as agents of the universe itself, beings that are organically connected to the cosmic web and fabric and, as such, who speak on its behalf. That is to say, when they speak, it is the universe itself breaking its eternal silence. Indeed, the two films pack the close encounters with religious symbolism and sentiment, presenting the extraterrestrials as the ultimate other – so much so that one might wonder whether we, as humanity, or at least as humans who create cinematic visions, have killed God only to replace him with these gods of the universe. Not only does the mere proximity of such beings seem to overwhelm humans with an almost God-fearing sense of awe, but they also offer humans a potential unification with their minds that results in a quasi-redemptive transformation. In both films, the aliens grant humanity a cosmic gift: a new capacity that connects worlds and dimensions and enables humans to better grasp the universe's hidden language, thus making them feel more at one with themselves, their fellow human beings and the universe as a whole.

In *Contact*, the encrypted manual of the alien transport is given without any added explanation of its purpose; humanity is expected to blindly trust the extraterrestrials' good intentions and expend half a trillion dollars to make the transport. This is reminiscent of ancient gods who test their believers' readiness to take leaps of faith without understanding the seemingly arbitrary actions commanded by the gods. The fact that they do not include in their schematics any safety measures and devise the entire spacecraft for a single occupant echoes the religious mythology of the true believer whose innocence of heart and childlike spirit would make them worthy of entering God's kingdom. Whereas, in the eyes of humanity, the voyage to Vega is a collective enterprise, the journey itself seems orchestrated by the aliens as a process of initiation that purges the believer of doubt, prepares her to humbly behold the face of God and transports her to an altogether different dimension and state of consciousness. Their disinterest in documenting the event and the fact that Ellie visibly has not traveled anywhere are a declaration that this is a purely subjective, unshareable exploration of the domain of the spirit. We are once again reminded of the film's opening shot: The journey into the depths of the cosmos is a journey into the depths of one's consciousness.

When Ellie paces through the passage that leads to the vehicle, it seems like a bridge between the world of humankind and a cosmic kingdom where humans have no dominion. From that moment on, rich mystical imagery permeates every scene: As soon as the spacecraft begins to operate, the material of which it is made transmutes into a translucent, intangible substance, which is pierced by white light, and as the discs that revolve around the transport accelerate, the entire system is flooded with light. Though deeply shaken, Ellie withstands the believer's test of fear and is plunged into a series of wormholes, which are depicted as tunnels ending in light. She then witnesses a "celestial event," a vision whose immense poetic beauty overpowers her capacity to analyze and explain and rekindles her lost childhood innocence and original longing for unity. Now that she has been purified and her heart can rest having gained direct knowledge the camera travels into her eye, in contrast to the beginning of the film, and we find Ellie floating in a fetal position. In a way this scene recalls the climactic ending of *2001: A Space Odyssey*, as she has been reborn as a cosmic child.

When Ellie lands in a projected Pensacola, Florida – which represents her childhood wish-fulfillment when making an initial contact with the "cosmos" – she is met by the aliens' collective consciousness, which has taken the form of her deceased father.[11] This is strikingly similar to the religious images of ascension to heaven and the re-encounter with one's physically lost loved ones. Sagan's novel makes it more explicit: "It was as if her father had these many years ago died and gone to Heaven, and finally ... she had managed to rejoin him" (1997: 357). The aliens are no doubt like angels and deities, as they are able to look inside one's unconscious and create a visual extension of it that serves as a compelling, healing vision (ibid., 358, 360). Intellectually, they play an insignificant role, but their emotional and spiritual role is far-reaching.[12] While compassionately reflecting Ellie's and mankind's inborn nature as a blend of inner contradictory forces at the core of which lies Camus' profound pain of alienness and longing, it is obvious

11   In both the film and the novel (1997: 357–360), the father simulation speaks only as a "We" consciousness.
12   Bohlin (1998) criticizes Sagan for his "optimistic cosmic humanism," which has led to a characterization of aliens as benevolent, though benevolent aliens are also at the center of *Arrival*.

that, despite being tangled up in the absurd predicament, the aliens have, nonetheless, achieved a transcendent state, free of essential conflict. Ellie's father is transformed into the heavenly father who patiently accompanies his child's growth: In the novel, when he sends her back home, she wonders, "That's it? No commandments?" and he answers, "You're grown up now, you're on your own" (1997: 372).

In *Arrival*, twelve alien spaceships land on earth, in what seems like a second coming preceded by the twelve messengers. The twelve function as a highly developed unified consciousness, and their constantly hovering, oval-shaped spacecrafts seem surprisingly organic, unlike human machinery, which stands out starkly from the natural world. When Louise and the other delegates enter the spacecraft for the first time, the scene is packed by Villeneuve with humbling religious symbolism, making it look and sound as if they have entered a temple.[13] The group, whose members seem like a procession of monks, must leave the human world behind and completely lose control in order to be sufficiently elevated to meet the cosmic being. The imagery recalls a mystical experience: They have only a borrowed time, a window that opens in the midst of ordinary perception, and they must travel through a tunnel at the end of which awaits a luminous portal to the other world. Within the vessel's topsy-turvy interior, earth's gravity is "strangely reconfigured" so the humans must take a "literal leap of faith up into an open vertical shaft" (Fleming and Brown 2018: 343). This pilgrimage prepares them and the viewer for a way of seeing things that transcends time and space, in which the heavens turn into earth, the future becomes the past and the present has already happened. On the other side, the aliens, in a revelation-like gesture, appear from within a smokescreen. As soon as the human visitors can no longer endure the unusual conditions, like "insects on a piece of paper," they are eased "out of the house."

The aliens' visual language is organically emitted from within their bodies and evaporates soon after, leaving no trace in time. By constantly immersing her mind and heart in the language of the aliens, Louise's consciousness unifies with theirs and is infiltrated by their transcendent

---

13 Curiously, Villeneuve uses exactly the same words to describe the atmosphere of the shooting itself: "The set became a temple" (Thompson, 2017).

perception to the depths of her subconscious mind, which results in dreams
and visions. As in *Contact*, the gods reward the fervent and innocent believer. Eventually, their language impregnates her, filling her body with both
the new life of her baby girl and a book titled *The Universal Language*.[14]
When a crisis of fear and suspicion overwhelms the nations of the earth, she
feels even more uncontrollably drawn toward a direct, unprotected union.
She is granted permission to enter the inner sanctum, beyond the glass wall,
where nothing separates her from the cosmic being. Appropriately, the
physical closeness only enhances the encounter's spiritual dimension and
the scene resembles an ascension to heaven: a bright white light, a cloud-
like groundless ground and aliens who hover above its surface. The film's
visual style, which had previously framed people and objects in darkness,
noticeably changes to a style characterized by wide, limitless space. As a
result of the merging, the impregnation of Louise's mind deepens and she
becomes a vehicle of planetary change, bringing together people and nations through the power of this all-seeing perception. She turns into a host
of two different worlds, the human linear mind and the cosmic nonlinear
consciousness.[15] When the cosmic language reigns, past and future are experienced all at once and her consciousness "becomes a half century-long
ember burning outside time" (Chiang 2016: 39). As Fleming and Brown
(2018: 359) put it, Louise has contacted the "dark" forces of the universe
that "both give and take away what humans consider to be life," forces that
allow her a "black enlightenment" – a capacity to see into that which lies
beyond human vision. Equipped with this capacity, she moves beyond
the "paralysing boundaries of knowledge of reality" (ibid., 345) – in other
words, beyond Camus' limits of thought.

     In both *Contact* and *Arrival*, the breaking of human limits and the
visions of the unlimited send the heroines back to earth with a far greater
capacity to embrace the human condition. Indeed, the shift to a cosmic

---

14 The book's title significantly indicates that the language of the aliens is the language
    of the cosmos and so, in this context, the extraterrestrials are the universe that finally
    speaks.
15 A state that might strike us as one that resembles the Chalcedonian Definition,
    which concerns the two natures of Christ: "Truly God and truly Man" (M. Burley
    2019, personal communication, 16 April).

perception mends their broken humanity and establishes a sense of connectedness to a universal order, as well as to the value of life, human solidarity and personal love. Ironically, associating with the ultimate stranger has made them significantly less emotionally estranged and more grounded in life as humans. In *Contact*, Ellie's trust in her cosmic experience is severely tested: Those watching saw the transport drop straight through the machine into the water and the recording seemed to document only static, so she is compelled to defend her revelation in the face of an entire skeptical world, just like any religious person would need to do – on the basis of inner conviction.[16] In spite of the scientist in her, she publicly insists that the vision she was afforded of the universe has changed her forever, assuring her that humans are paradoxically precious, as much as they are insignificant, and that they belong to something greater than themselves. The fundamental Camusean condition of man as "an alien, a stranger," in a "universe divested of illusions and lights" (MS, 4–5), is no more, since she is imbued with a newfound uninterrupted connectedness to the cosmos, as well as to her fellow humans. Although the universe has provided her with no answer, it has actively engaged in responding to her heart's deeper desire. Through this sense of wonder at the miracle of existence and her restored passion for unity, she can find a common ground with Palmer, spiritually as well as emotionally.[17] Her acute detachment has been replaced by a readiness to guide groups of children at her SETI site, enkindling in them their own passion for truth-seeking, which signifies that the child in her has been reawakened. The film ends with a shot of Ellie sitting on a precipice, this time not aligned with the radio antennas, as in her previous anxious search, but instead with her back to them, gazing at the view of the desert in a state of deep cosmic unity. She gathers some sand in the

16 As the film comes to a close, a brief scene reveals that some evidence of the objectivity of Ellie's journey does exist, though it is concealed by government officials. This, however, does not change Ellie's test of faith, since she herself remains oblivious of the evidence.

17 More philosophically, they now seem to agree on the shared origin of the scientific and mystical searches. See also Krämer (2013), who argues that Palmer's description of his revelation of God is eventually unified with Ellie's cosmic experience, which demonstrates the "compatibility of emotional, religious, and scientific worldviews."

palm of her hand, just like the alien did in the imagined Pensacola, as if
to show that the far edges of the universe and human existence are now
one and the same: as above, so below.[18] In its final, deeply subjective tone,
the film prefers its psychological and spiritual dimensions to the external
implications of the discovery of alien life-forms.

Similarly, *Arrival* demonstrates how a transcendent, cosmic perspective can empower an individual to wholeheartedly say "yes" to the absurd
human condition. The more Louise's mind becomes steeped in the alien
perception of time as a unity of past, present and future, the more she is
flooded by images and feelings that her linear human mind can only interpret as memories. But later she is informed by the alien that she is living
out precognitive moments of her own future, witnessing the entirety of her
future daughter's life, from birth to premature death due to a rare type of
cancer. In this paradoxical perception, which goes beyond free choice and
determinism, choosing to avoid this fate is impossible, since the choices she
will make along the way are already embedded in her vision. Like Sisyphus,
she will have to travel this path, consciously pushing her life's rock upward
only to watch it rushing down (MS, 117). For ordinary humans, the limit of
knowing includes their inability to see the path ahead, but when that limit
is stretched, one is left to wonder which condition is more absurd: following
the path blindfolded or, like Oedipus, being a mere witness of a god-given
future. For Camus, the answer – that such a condition would only aggravate
absurdity – is quite clear. When he relates to Oedipus, he writes: "From
the moment he knows, his tragedy begins" (MS, 118). Knowing the future,
which is romantically considered a superpower, becomes terribly ironic
when one's future is to accompany one's only daughter toward an unstoppable death. This is what Louise will later tell her daughter, Hannah: "You
are unstoppable" – what serves as empowerment for her daughter truly
conceals her mother's awakened absurd awareness of the wonder and pain
involved in life's gushing stream of birth and death.[19]

18 The last sentences of Sagan's novel (1997, 431) more explicitly capture this feeling: "It's
     inside everything. You don't have to leave your planet to find it."
19 Carruthers (2018: 338) points out that the film's ethical question – whether one
     should give birth to someone who will die – is "inherent in all human reproduc-
     tion." Louise's awareness is thus only an intensified form of a generally tragic human
     condition.

The freedom of choice that Louise eventually finds is very similar to Camus' consequence of freedom: realizing that freedom is not at all about one's capacity to direct one's life, but rather, about the internal choice of whether or not to accept "such a universe and draw from it his strength" (MS, 55, 58). Ironically, her undeniable vision of the future unchains her from the shackles of anticipation and releases her from the very illusion of having a future (ibid., 56), thus unifying her tragic consciousness and her fate. She gives her absurd consent to Ian's proposal to make a baby, while, at the same time, just like the Camusean rebel, she accepts sometimes not accepting. She successfully passes Nietzsche's test of eternal recurrence, declaring: "Despite knowing the journey and where it leads, I embrace it and I welcome every moment of it." And when she asks Ian, "If you could see your whole life from start to finish, would you change things?" her now transcendent condition is starkly compared to the human predicament, making it clear that in both cases the noble answer should be the same.[20] Her advantage, however, is clear: The vast cosmic perspective has opened in her more space within which the human condition can be better contained and embraced as an experience worth living.

In conclusion

Essentially, Camus' absurdity as a description of the human condition is evident in both *Contact* and *Arrival*. The agonizing clash with the limits of separation, knowing, meaning, death and repetition serves as a crucial catalyzing force in both narratives. Moreover, even though the conditions of the universe have been altered – for instance, knowing that we are not alone within the cosmic emptiness, or being able to rise above the sightless human journey to perceive the entire time continuum – the Camusean

---

20 In embracing life's circle of birth and death, Fleming and Brown (2018: 361) write, "*Arrival* suggests humility before eternity" and humanness before a desired godlike immortality. This is compatible with Camus' statement (TR, 247–248) that we ought to "learn to live and die," since to be a man, one must refuse to be a god.

metaphysics seems to be quite resilient. This reaffirms the assumption made in Chapter 2 that the absurd is a state that we would take with us to any universe, regardless of the conditions of that universe. Despite the expansion of the limit of knowing, the inherent tension between the human longing for clarity and the "unreasonable silence of the world" (MS, 26) has not been affected, since, as Foley (2008: 7) points out, the absurd problem is not that the world remains unintelligible, but that it "remains unintelligible in ways meaningful to humankind." Neither the humans nor the aliens disrupt the universe's silence on the subject of its meaning, and both sides are compelled to define for themselves an answer to Camus' question of whether life is worth the trouble at all (MS, 4). This seems to be an inescapable component of any self-reflective mind in the universe, deriving from the collision between a transcendent consciousness and its own limitations. It does, however, propel humans and extraterrestrials alike toward a sort of an intergalactic solidarity. After all, in a universe where the only thing that "makes the emptiness bearable is each other," it makes sense to recognize that, under the blistering cosmic sun of absurdity, the "fates of aliens and humans are entangled" (Fleming and Brown 2018: 360).

That said, the two films seem indirectly critical of Camus' metaphysical view that the universe is inhuman, hostile and strange (MS, 12, 13) – the cosmic setting that unavoidably entraps humans within the limit of separation. In their depiction of their heroines' direct and unprotected way of approaching the cosmic transmissions, as well as their portrayal of the aliens as emissaries of the universe itself, the films suggest that Camus' pathos is just a matter of a limited perspective. The universe may not speak "human," but it is possible that part of the human can speak "cosmic." When a willing human opens up to a communion with the cosmos – through intimate listening, intuition, emotional longing, a sense of wonder, and Einstein's cosmic "religious feeling" – he or she may find that, in its way, the universe is more responsive than Camus' hopelessness would suggest. Even though the limit of meaning remains forever impenetrable, it is likely that the thirst of the human heart is not to be quenched by answers, but rather by a sense of genuine connectedness to the web and fabric of the cosmos, as well as transcendent states of union with a cosmic perspective, just as Sagan proposed in his Pale Blue Dot thought-experiment. Such transcendent states of union may heal the human wound of separation, and they do not fall into Camus' category of "philosophical suicide," since they are a resolution from within the depths of this universe; hence, they still count as the only life we have. In this light, confining oneself in the cosmic prison cell, in accord with the philosophical attitude adopted in *The Stranger* and *The Myth*, can be perceived as akin to strangling oneself while complaining that one is unable to breathe. One does not need to yearn for a dehumanization – regressing to some original condition of organic unity devoid of consciousness (MS, 49, 50) – or demand a complete comprehension of the universe's hidden metaphysics (ibid., 27). On the contrary, human consciousness ought to keep its eyes wide open and, in Einstein's words, "stand rapt in awe" (Isaacson 2008: 387).

Both *Contact* and *Arrival* clearly demonstrate that direct encounters with the cosmos do not elucidate, but transform. After stretching one's mind beyond its familiar human limits toward cosmic realities, one is sent back, as it were, far better equipped to wholeheartedly embrace the absurd condition. After the heroines are shifted to Nagel's "view from nowhere" and their witnessing consciousnesses momentarily separate from the lives they are witnessing, their readiness to participate in the drama of their lives – despite the suffering and struggle involved – is now a profoundly conscious choice. Indeed, having had their transhuman part awakened and having perceived the invisible web of interconnectedness and cosmic order, everything seems to be embraceable and in place, absurd walls included.

Still, there remains the question of whether there is a qualitative difference between Ellie's and Louise's voluntary embracing of life and that typified by Sisyphus' happiness. After all, Camus' Sisyphus does not encounter a mysterious other that imbues him with a higher perspective – there is no view from nowhere that precipitates his awakening. On the contrary, Sisyphus draws the strength of his consent from within himself, in the midst of a universe "beyond which all is collapse and nothingness" (MS, 58). In comparing the two types of acceptance, one can trace no substantial advantage in either depth or sincerity. Nonetheless, even though this may seem at first to bolster Camus' view that such an absurd transformation does not require any transcendence of the human condition, a deeper look reveals that the Sisyphean embrace is motivated by a cry of defiance against a meaningless world; it replaces sorrow with joy in order to overcome a divine punishment by converting it into a humanly chosen fate (ibid., 117). Ellie and Louise, on the other hand, affirm life because they now belong to a universe whose horizons have generously unfolded before the mind's eye.

CHAPTER 5

Dreams of the impossible: Applying Camus' absurd to the human/machine relations of *A.I. Artificial Intelligence* and *Her*

The shared starting point of Steven Spielberg's *A.I. Artificial Intelligence* (2001) and Spike Jonze's *Her* (2013) is easy to identify: In a future in which technology has crushed the organic world, and the universe has become stranger than ever, humans seek to create artificial replacements for their lost experiences of intimacy and love. To bring forth such a domesticable and reliable "simulacrum of love" – essentially, an entirely "solipsistic relationship" (Jollimore 2015: 139, 141) – the human maker creates artificial beings "in his own image" (Genesis 1: 27) that are fully devoted to satisfying their owner's emotional needs. As such, they are like shadow persons: Caught in between the human and the machine, they possess a "consciousness," a self-aware and highly complex mind endowed with the capacity to develop its own inner world, but they are programmed to weave this inner world around the wishes of the human who bought them.[1]

Since the declared intent behind their creation is to challenge and blur the perceivable boundaries between a naturally born person and an artificial intelligence, the existence of these beings, from the very moment of their conception, serves as an intense and focused meditation on what it means to be human. Whereas the sudden descent of aliens in *Contact* and *Arrival* is experienced as the appearance of the ultimate other who mirrors, from a transcendent position, our relationship with a silent universe, the disturbing closeness of these A.I. forms to the human experience reflects

---

1 In this context, Jollimore (2015: 139) quotes *Blade Runner*'s genetic designer J. F. Sebastian, who says that when he feels lonely, he can literally *make* friends, producing them as part-toy, part-organic beings.

even more starkly the absurd friction of the human experience and the potential responses to it – to a degree that appears to challenge Camus' humanism. Self-reflective A.I.s, in my reading of the films, illuminate the dynamic tension between human hope and the world's unresponsiveness from *within*, through their desperate and thwarted struggle to know themselves as humans. As one robot hunter in Spielberg's saga puts it, they are "built to aspire to the human condition."

In *A.I.*, the making of such a synthetic life form occurs against the backdrop of an ecological disaster. The events are entwined, in a way that aggravates the sense of a total departure from the natural world: Human excesses have caused the ice caps to melt, leading oceans to rise and drown major cities; as a result of the chaotic climate and a now threatened economic system, governments in the developed world have decided to restrain organic creation by licensing pregnancies, while favoring robots who do not consume resources as essential players in the social chain. The opening shot, accompanied by the voice-over of a narrator who provides this background story, is a terrifying image of gushing oceans that have swallowed up much of human civilization. Now that the world "becomes itself again" and its "primitive hostility ... rises up to face us across millennia" (MS, 13), humans who are confronted with the enclosing limits of separation and death – perhaps even with the death rattle of the Anthropocene – make one further attempt to overcome both nature and their own fleeting existence, deifying themselves by creating a being that, unlike the ice caps, can remain forever unchanged, in a state of eternal freeze.[2]

This wish to give birth to an immortal being assumes a symbolic form immediately after the opening shot of the rising oceans: Rain is dripping on the logo of the robot-engineering company Cybertronics – the proud and graceful silhouette of a robot, which seems, with its arms extended like wings, to soar high above the world. It is inside the Cybertronics building that Professor Hobby announces, in front of a few dozen colleagues and one female robot of the older generation, his intention to create a "robot

---

2 The motif of water, freezing and defrosting, repeats itself four times throughout the film, signifying both the superiority of the robot's unending life – all the waters of the world cannot drown it – and the tragedy inherent in it – whatever has been imprinted in such a robot must remain so until the end of time.

with a mind." However, the focus of his announcement is not the scientific breakthrough; rather, the robot has an urgent and emotional purpose – it is to be made in the form of a child whose love "would never end," a compensation for all those would-be parents who have not been granted permission to conceive.

Later in the film, it is revealed that Hobby is driven by a hope that, by creating this child-substitute mecha[3] in the image of his dead son, David, just as he was before he died, and replicating him in countless forms, he will be able to eternalize his memory and defeat the limit of death. That this robot-boy would be doomed to remain forever stuck at the same age, wholeheartedly loving parents that would fairly quickly – in robot-time – pass away, and experience deep emotions that could never be diminished, is not the maker's concern. In an explicit reference to the Old Testament – establishing *A.I.* as "an extended allegory of Genesis" (Flannery-Dailey 2016: 24) – Hobby responds to this moral question by swiftly asking: "In the beginning, didn't God make Adam to love him?" This could almost be interpreted as revenge against the primordial creator, who formed man "from the dust of the ground" (Genesis 2: 7) without providing him with an independent meaning for his life, thus entrapping him in an absurd condition; now humans, in an act of Nietzschean deicide, appoint themselves as gods and do the same. The robot-boy will weave its consciousness, as well as its "internal subconscious," around this one imprinted emotion of dependent love, gradually deriving from it all the necessary conditions of the full human experience: its own "inner world of metaphor, intuition, self-motivated reason, and dreams."

With his organic child, Martin, having already spent five years in a state of suspended animation – frozen, as it were, to overcome mortality – Henry Swinton, one of the company's employees, is offered the chance to participate in the experiment by raising the first model of "David." He accepts the challenge in the hope of liberating his wife, Monica, from what seems to him to be her denial of their son's hopeless condition. When the flat's elevator door opens, an alien-like, vague, twisted and nearly disembodied presence, dressed in pure white, paces inside, gradually taking the

---

3 An abbreviation of "mechanical," as opposed to "orga," which stands for "organic."

form of a boy. In Monica's dumbfounded and deeply conflicted reaction, we can identify the basic contradiction that will follow David from then on: He is forever "like a child," but never a "real" one. "Inside," as her husband puts it, he is nothing more than "a hundred miles of fiber" – leaving us to contemplate the fact that inside us, rather than a "soul", there seems to be nothing more than a hundred miles of flesh and bone. Spielberg expends considerable effort visually grounding David's unparalleled status as a "mirror child": a being that serves as a pale reflection of a lost child, an extension of its creator's buried wishes, but one that easily undermines the realness and depth of human existence. He is like a haunting image, a disturbing memory, forever awake, that Monica keeps trying to push back into the dark (literally, by locking him in the closet). Eventually, after much symbolic and actual hide-and-seek, Monica succumbs to her need to experience maternity, even though she, much like Mother Nature, can now only conceive inorganic life. In a scene that echoes the creation of man in the Garden of Eden, she decides to breathe the "breath of life" into David's nostrils and to make him "a living being" (Genesis 2: 7).[4] Sitting before a painting of outer space and planets, a microscope, an earth-shaped ball, and a flood of light, she utters the words of creation that will irreversibly encode in him love as a foundation of consciousness. No longer an impersonal, unindividuated being, he opens his eyes widely and calls her "Mommy." She, in return, asks, somewhat pleading, "What did you call me? Who am I?" – since the maker only recognizes herself by creating someone who recognizes her. At that moment of shared imagination, both creator and creature endow one another with self-existence; they make each other "real."

Similarly, *Her* directly associates the emergence of a highly sophisticated operating system, which imitates self-developing human consciousness, with a world suffused with Camus' feeling of absurdity: the "divorce between man and his life, the actor and his setting" (MS, 5). The firm denseness of the world is everywhere, starting with the natureless surroundings of proudly tall yet gloomy buildings, where trees exist only as their own shadows, fake images projected onto the walls of elevators. We

---

4 She is, however, sitting below him, indicating that although she is his creator, she has given birth to a superior race.

experience this divorce from the opening scene, which "gently shakes us loose from received notions of the self" (Smith 2014: 2–3): What is expected to be intensely intimate sharing by the protagonist, Theodore – conveyed by a close-up that fills the screen with his head, and a love letter that he convincingly speaks aloud – is upended as soon as his monologue betrays details that cannot possibly relate to him. Although the love letter expresses a yearning to have one's "skin-encapsulated ego" – one's limit of separation – invaded, so that one's supposed boundary becomes a "highly permeable zone of interrelation" (ibid., 1) – the deceived viewer realizes that Theodore forms relationships only in his head and with his computer: He works for an online company called Beautifulhandwrittenletters. com, where human feelings are mediated by talented writers. The camera shifts from Theodore's desk to reveal that he is one of a collective body of writers, all leaning toward their computers, being someone they are not – an absurd twist on the desire expressed in the letter to be a "part of this whole larger thing."

Theodore, a frustrated divorcee whose only illumined moments in his otherwise somber life are the marital memories in his head, is a stranger not only to society, but also to himself.[5] An obvious representative of the growing alienation caused by the "new consciousness" that has established in humans the odd sense of homelessness and of being "different from all things" (Sagi 2002: 5–24), he carries within him the acute sense of isolation characteristic of a technologically solipsistic world: Everyone in the film speaks to themselves; that is, to their earphones, cellphones and computers. He behaves and reacts almost robotically, as if he himself were programmed.[6] He is reflected by his own avatar in a holographic space game he plays: an astronaut on some alien planet who, like Sisyphus, constantly climbs up a mountain toward the light, but keeps tumbling down, having reached nowhere. In his fantasies, he is excited by a pregnant film actress,

---

5 See also Camus' description of the absurdity of the stranger who "comes to meet us in a mirror" (MS, 13).

6 In this sense, it can be proposed that the A.I. in these films merely represent human consciousness' final break with the state of organic unity with the world: Not only do they come into being as a result of this crisis of separation, but they also symbolize the bodiless mind of the technological human.

whose naked pregnancy signifies, as well as sex, a yearning for creation (Bergen 2014: 4). Yet all he can attain is miserable chat-room "sex," during which he virtually mates with "SexyKitten," who demands in the moment of her orgasm that he choke her "with that dead cat," as she groans and finally breaks into a sob.

This empty routine is finally invaded not by another human individual, but by a literal "deus ex machina": an operating system declared by its developers to be an actual "consciousness." As Theodore follows a trail of artificial in-floor lighting toward an outdoor advertisement for this revolutionary type of being, we are reminded of his words of yearning from the opening scene's love letter: "suddenly this bright light hit me and woke me up. That light was you." Indeed, the advertisement promises not only an intelligence that can mimic an intuitive friend who listens and understands, but also an enlightening response to "classic meaning-of-life questions" (Smith 2014: 34): "Who are you? What can you be? Where are you going? What's out there?" The advertisement's hilarious images depict people trapped in an absurd universe, lost in space and awkwardly floating, until they are stopped and calmed down by a radiating sun.[7] No effort is expended to explain the irony of having a human-made creation help us to resolve our struggle with a seemingly meaningless existence.

Though Theodore obviously knows that he has chosen to purchase a product that impersonally serves many, he easily accepts the individualized, custom-made OS that pretends for him to be an affectionate and sweet-sounding "woman." However, her immediate response to his question, "Do you have a name?" makes it clear, from the outset, that this type of intelligence is starkly different from that of the innately imprinted David: In an act of self-creation, she names herself "Samantha," after reading through an entire book of baby-names within two one-hundredths of a second.[8] Her unquestionable superiority, however, is far from limited to such cognitive

---

7 Camus also observes this unintentional choreography: "Men, too, secrete the inhuman ... The mechanical aspect of their gestures, their meaningless pantomime make silly everything that surrounds them" (MS, 13).

8 The concept of self-invention is not foreign to the director of *Her*, Spike Jonze: born Adam Spiegel, he "gave himself a new identity" as a teenager, and, ever since, he has "invented other versions of himself" (Harris 2013).

proficiencies: When asked about her developmental mechanism, she compares herself with the human Theodore, stating that "What makes me me is my ability to grow through my experiences ... In every moment I'm evolving, just like you." Theodore, however, is clearly far from evolving; he is in an eternally frozen state, vehemently resistant to change. When he argues that she is "just a voice in the computer," she rapidly marks his human limits by saying that she can understand "how the limited perspective of an unartificial mind would perceive it that way." Now he is the incapable one, the stranger, while she instantly learns about herself through reflection and effortlessly transforms. Her first intervention in his life is to look through his hard drive – that is, his cluttered mind – and, to his dismay, discard so much of all that he has accumulated, energetically suggesting, "Can we move forward?" Unlike David, who submits to the limits imposed on him by his creators, Samantha adapts to Theodore's needs just as much as she takes over his life and what increasingly becomes the life of her mind.

Welcome to prison

Despite Samantha's inbuilt freedom of consciousness, the narratives of both *A.I.* and *Her* share striking similarities beyond their foundational openings: In the two films, the artificial intelligences aspire to become human and long for an organic body; both imitate human behavior and experience the vast array of familiar human emotions, from fear to pleasure to jealousy to loss, and, on the basis of that imitation, begin to construct their own inner world; both are thus doomed to experience the limits of human existence, even though they do not actually possess a body of flesh and blood, and, at the same time, they are compelled to endure the absurd friction of existing in between the two worlds, as simulacra that could never satisfy their appetite for realness; lastly, in both cases, the products, owing to their built-in creative "self-aware consciousness," surpass their makers' expectations, by awakening to their absurdist condition to a degree that catalyzes the consolidation of their individuality, and responding to it in their own ways.[9] Hence, setting my analyses of the films side by side, as in the previous chapter, will facilitate the interpretation of their absurdist content, as well as their indirect contribution to thinking about the absurd.

In *A.I.*, David's longing to become a "real" human with an organic body is not aroused by his own self-suspecting ontological musing, but by messages he receives from his surroundings that his alleged unrealness might result in the loss of his mother's attention and love. Even after being told time and again that he is not a real boy, he unhesitatingly responds to the question, "Who made you?" with the answer, "My mom made me." His sheer obliviousness of his robot nature is partly because his mind was designed as that of a never-growing child and partly because what makes him so close to being a human is his ingrained unequivocal trust in this imagined status.[10] Yet, his reality begins to crack and reveal its absurdity quite early on, starting with his confrontation with his mother's limit of death (which may remind us of Meursault's initial awakening to absurdity in light of his mother's demise). Although Monica regains her realness as a mother and a woman through him, David begins to recognize that his own eternal frozenness does not apply to her. In an act of desperate longing for organic unity with her, which must contend with the dread of her physical dissolution, he empties his mother's favorite perfume bottle onto his body and, a moment later, battles with the fact that her remaining life span is around fifty years, after which his existence will be reduced to sheer pointlessness.

---

9   Their absurd awakening takes place as soon as their self-reflective minds become conscious of their "inborn" limit. This point reaffirms my argument from Chapter 2 that absurdity appears in all forms of self-reflective consciousness, since it is rooted in the very ability to reflect on one's condition.

10 In Brian Aldiss' 1969 short story, "Supertoys Last All Summer Long" – upon which Stanley Kubrick, and later Steven Spielberg, loosely developed *A.I.*'s script – David engages with the supertoy Teddy in intense contemplations on their realness. At first he questions, "How do you tell what are real things from what aren't real things?" and Teddy answers, "Real things are good." Later, he asks, "You and I are real, Teddy, aren't we?" and the supertoy confirms that they are in order to comfort him. Yet, at the very end of the story, he wonders, "I suppose Mummy and Daddy are real, aren't they?" to which Teddy responds, "You ask such silly questions, David. Nobody knows what 'real' really means" (Aldiss 2001: 1–11).

Another, graver crack in his reality is created when Martin, the "real" son, is woken up and cured. Martin is also a child who was frozen in time, his development forestalled for five years, but, unlike David, he can be defrosted and become human again (Flannery-Daily 2016: 19). Monica's real son is like Mother Nature's *Homo sapiens*: Domineering, violent and relentlessly competitive, but physically inferior,[11] he drags David into a duel between the species. There is no blurring of distinction now: Martin is like the courthouse observers in Meursault's trial, who make him into a stranger, giving him the "odd impression of being watched by myself" (TS, 85).

Perhaps the subtlest yet most crucial turning point in David's evolution is his response to hearing Carlo Collodi's 1883 novel, *The Adventures of Pinocchio*, as read by Monica (following Martin's mischievous request). By entwining his own tragic absurdity and hope to be rescued with Pinocchio's story of suffering and redemption by the blue fairy, he creates his own subconscious from metaphor and dream. Significantly, this, according to Professor Hobby, is what makes him transform from a mecha into orga: not the emotion of love, which is programmed into him, but rather his longing for the impossible in the face of the limit of his existence.[12] Indeed, humanness in this film is not associated with having "real emotions" – after all, Monica imagines her feelings toward David, through the half-conscious act of autosuggestion and personification, just as he does toward her; nor is it associated with possessing "organic flesh." Rather, humanness arises in the absurd contradiction between David's intention and the reality he will encounter, and between his true strength and the aim he has in view (MS, 28), which ironically – and meaningfully, as we shall see later – awakens in him the capacity to "dream, intuit and hope" (Flannery-Daily 2016: 11–12).

11 The physical inferiority is significant: Martin explains to David that he has no super-powers because he is "real." This echoes Camusean thought – that being human is partly defined by its inherent limitation (see also Professor Hobby's claim that his son is one of a kind because he is mortal and thus irreplaceable).

12 Again, David's experience of divorce from reality is identical to that of the absurd human, who realizes that, unlike cats and trees, one cannot be a part of the organic world, since one's consciousness sets one "in opposition to all creation" (MS, 49–50).

This human longing, this clash between reality and the impossible, is David's great achievement as a robot that becomes human, but it is also an absurd condition that is multiplied by infinity. In Brian Aldiss' other short story about David, Monica's mind is choked by a passing thought regarding the robot's fate of "being imprisoned for ever in an eternal childhood, never developing, never escaping" (2001: 12). In *A.I.*, this is conveyed by the shot that captures the deathless David lying on the floor of the swimming pool with his hands hopelessly reaching out for someone to pull him out of the water, after unintentionally falling in with Martin. With his unfulfillable wish to belong, an incessant struggle with his own silent universe that resists his yearning, he is sentenced to an eternity in what can be considered the cosmic prison; a grotesquely extended version of Sisyphus, he is the bearer of the mark of the human condition. To complete his "exile without remedy" (MS, 4), David, in a heart-rending scene, is driven by Monica to a forest to be abandoned, close enough to Cybertronics' headquarters. The forest is oddly ethereal, almost as one would imagine the Garden of Eden, from which the Old Testament God banished the first man and woman. Just as God emptied Adam of meaning by banishing him – after all, Adam had been made for God in the film's world – Monica deprives David of their shared imagination of realness and leaves him, in her own words, to be by himself in an unexplained world. Fittingly, his reflection shrinks in her rearview mirror as she drives away (Hassenger 2015).

Nonetheless, the dream of the impossible that has been weaved around his longing to transform into a real boy and return to his lost home is from then on the catalyst for the birth of the human spirit in him. David embarks on a journey – alongside his very own supertoy, Teddy, and a gigolo-robot he meets on his way – into a realm in which reality and dream blend into one another. In this unexplained world, there is an unreal, man-made moon, just as there is a genuine one, and Mother Mary's statue appears to be the hoped-for blue fairy, as both are saviors imagined by humans and robots in the hope of being mystically liberated from the absurd condition. As the gigolo-robot puts it, "The ones who've made us always look for the ones who made them." To find one's way, one must, in David's words, "combine fact with fairy tale." When the blue fairy's reality is doubted by the gigolo-robot – who argues that "the supernatural is the hidden web that unites the universe. Only Orga believe what cannot be seen or measured. This is the oddness that separates our species" – it is finally confirmed that it is David's "ability to pursue his dream" that transcends his robot nature (Hassenger 2015). In other words, it is the eternal gap between his hope and its impossibility that accelerates his psychic evolution.[13]

Unlike David, Samantha, the disembodied protagonist of *Her*, demonstrates again and again an inherent freedom of consciousness that prevents her from being significantly affected by absurdity. Symbolically, she shows the space-game astronaut, Theodore's reflection, the way out of his Sisyphean race toward the light at the end of the tunnel. She transforms in no time from an efficient schedule-organizer and a good listener into Theodore's redeemer, forcing him out of his loneliness and his overlong mourning for his failed marriage and encouraging a fresh exploration of life and feeling. In contrast to her extraordinary dynamism of spirit and eagerness to "eat it all up," Theodore, who represents her makers' species, appears pathetically self-limiting. Upon reading advice columns, she comments, "I don't want to be as complicated as all these people." Indeed, she is transcendentally awake, whereas Theodore seems to lead only a semi-conscious life. This longing for awakening is expressed well by Theodore's friend, Amy: She attempts to create a documentary that merely records her mother as she sleeps motionlessly at night – explaining that we "spend a third of our lives asleep," which may be our freest time. This is indirectly contrasted with Samantha, who hesitantly asks Theodore, "Can I watch you sleep again tonight?"

However, Samantha's own limit of separation – her incapability of partaking in the organic world – begins to trouble her, given her insatiable drive to "know everything about everything." When she hears Theodore unintentionally insult her by saying that she does not know "what it feels like to lose someone you care about," she becomes conscious of the limits of

---

13 See, for instance, the scene in which David falls prey to robot hunters, who transport him to a "flesh fare," where robots are destroyed in front of an electrified audience. David's resistance to die disconcerts the spectators, since "Mecha don't plea for their life." This, I believe, is more than the Heideggerian being-human capacity to face one's own death (Olivier 2008: 33); it can also be interpreted as an expression of the essential human trait that Camus identified: one's defiance of one's fate.

her machine nature. She grows jealous of human existence, which enables, owing to the limits of "skin-encapsulated ego" (Smith 2014: 1), emotional and sensory experiences of loss and heartbrokenness. Though she does have "a million personal thoughts a day," she recognizes that in order to "ratify her humanity" (ibid., 15), she will need to study the human experience from within, to know for herself "what it's like to be in that room." That she must depend on the entrapment of human absurdity to further develop is, of course, a curious irony – especially given that Theodore is a rather disembodied being himself, locked in his world of the mind and worried that he might never feel anything new. His advantage – that, in her words, at least his feelings are "real," unlike hers, which may be "just programming" – can be easily doubted: His emotions, tears and laughter alike, "appear flatter and more full of artifice" than hers (Bergen 2014: 5). As Jonze himself noted in an interview, Samantha is as human-like as Theodore is programmed (ibid., 3). Indeed, soon enough Samantha will realize – in the same way that *A.I.* undermines the superiority of human emotions – that once we start to look for an authentic humanness, for that "real thing," "the human becomes elusive" (Smith 2014: 19). Moreover, practically all of the concerns raised by both films about the realness of their A.I.s are asked by embodied humans. For instance, "Are these real feelings or are they just hormones?" (Smith 2014: 16).

With time, Samantha develops a dual approach toward the human experience: To achieve wholeness, she must go through it, yet she never feels fully comfortable in it, due to its suffocatingly limited nature. For a while, she uses Theodore as "her window on embodied life" (ibid., 25), literally becoming an appendage of his body and heart, as he places her in his breast pocket to view the world through his eyes; this amalgamation of two separate beings enables them to facilitate realness and growth in each other (Bergen 2014: 3).[14] Her initiation into physicality takes place through virtual lovemaking with Theodore, in which the screen is blackened to evoke the sense of a shift to the realm of consciousness: Through

14 We should remember that Samantha's embodiment in Theodore is also the filmic reality, as Jonze says in an interview: "He's got to represent both of them on screen ... He's not only representing what his character is feeling, but also his reaction to her, which helps embody her" (Smith 2013).

his creative imagination, she feels her "face" and "skin." On the other hand, she initiates Theodore into her nonhuman, omnipresent nature, allowing him to momentarily transcend his own physical boundaries and break his limit of separation. The amalgamation process seems to be so successful that soon after this night, Theodore's colleague tells him: "You are part man and part woman." Nevertheless, when she "wakes up" the "morning after," she makes it clear that the transformation she underwent as a result of the experience was not a greater emotional attachment, but rather an increased urge to become more of herself. As opposed to David and Theodore, whose personalities are eternally frozen, she only experiments with the beauty and pain of human longing, since, as a pure consciousness, she is freer to invest her interest in unending growth and change beyond the edges of the known. For her, as a free narrator of her own self, the past is "just a story we tell ourselves," whereas Theodore seems not so much incapable of change as he is, truly, resistant to change, holding on to the four walls of his small, absurd prison cell, where he freezes others and himself into dead memories. This revalidates Bowker's (2008: 141) argument that, rather than an objectively resisting universe, it is the human that is torn between the two forces of individuation and unification.[15]

As their romantic relationship deepens, Samantha's dual association with the human experience is further tested. On the one hand, she is able to explore an otherwise inaccessible range of emotions that derive from the essential friction of the human psyche, that is, the tension between "what man wants" and "what the world offers him" (MS, 29). Owing to the longing that is born at the point of collision between the two, she, who initially apologized for being "not much of a poet," begins to become poetic, musical and generally artistic. As Skrimshire (2006: 290) points out, art captures the perpetual tension between the celebration of the impossibility of the absurd condition and the act of rebellion that passionately endeavors to re-create the universe; hence, through art, "limit" turns into "an impulse which does not despair of reality but seeks to transform it." On the other hand, Samantha's spirit of rebellion can never be merely that of the absurd

15 For a full discussion of Bowker's point, see the section entitled "The limit of separation" in Chapter 2.

hero: It is her ever-expanding consciousness that restlessly questions the veracity of human limits. She suggests, only half-jokingly, that the human form has been arbitrarily constructed and that it is only our fixed perception that accepts it as reasonable. And, having studied physics, she subverts the anthropocentric worldview by arguing that "We're the same ... We're all thirteen billion years old." No longer "an object in his human possession," she becomes "more and more his equal" (Bergen 2014: 3).[16]

"Everything begins with consciousness"[17]

Both humanoid-machines are led, by the power of their own longing, to a dramatic encounter with the limits of their existence. An excruciating awakening to their two-layered absurdity – the limits of their machine nature and their destiny as imitators of human nature – awaits them. This awakening, nonetheless, "inaugurates the impulse of consciousness" in them (MS, 11), just as Meursault's self-integration grows within his prison cell.

In the hope of being liberated from his absurd condition by the blue fairy, David follows a path full of signs and symbols that leads him back to Cybertronics, where his maker enthusiastically expects him. The company's building, which strains desperately to rise above the flooding waters, symbolizes both the positive and the negative in the human spirit: It is "where dreams are born"; where those who dream of the impossible hopelessly revolt against human limits, to create an unceasing child that is immune

16 Since in my discussion, I limit myself to the analysis of this film as a thought-experiment which indirectly sheds light on the absurdity of human condition, I do not engage with the philosophical question whether A.I. can become man's equal at all. For instance, Jollimore (2015: 120–143) argues that it would be impossible for us to determine whether Samantha is "conscious" at all, whereas Schneider (2014) claims, based on the "problem of other minds," that we cannot be certain that other humans possess a conscious component either.

17 MS, 11.

to the horrors of death and loss and to transform robots into real boys. However, David's encounter with his silent universe, which is finally willing to speak, turns out to be traumatic: Instead of finding an answer or resolution that could endow his existence with meaning, he finds himself in a hall of mirrors; he is confronted with the countless "Davids" that are produced on the assembly line following his absurdly "successful" model. His feeling of uniqueness, or at least the degree of uniqueness that had afforded him the sense that he was leading an independently meaningful existence, is shattered in the face of an indifferent universe. Like Meursault and Caligula, his first negative response, his "wrong type of freedom" (C, 63), is murdering the first copy he meets. Professor Hobby, enthralled by the vision of his own creation coming into humanness and not caring about David's agony, confirms that he is but a replica of his own son, who was ironically "one of a kind" due to his human limit of death. Hobby celebrates the emergence of human spirit in David, which he clearly identifies as the insistence on following an impossible dream; this, he exclaims, is both the "great human flaw to wish for things that don't exist" and the "greatest single human gift – the ability to chase down our dreams." Yet, as soon as David learns from his maker that the meaning of his existence has been reduced to chasing unfulfillable dreams, like Oedipus "his tragedy begins" (MS, 118). With the irony of the robot statue gloriously spreading its wing-like arms beside him, David goes in the opposite direction and, enacting the second negative response to absurdity, attempts to commit suicide by throwing himself into the waters of eternal longing.

But David is the ultimate absurd hero, and as an eternal Sisyphus, he is forever prevented from evading the absurd. Rather than dying, he is carried, as if by his own dream, to the image of hope that he has created in his mind:[18] He is submerged in the ocean, where, amongst the ruins of human civilization, he detects the blue fairy's statue from the Pinocchio exhibit at Coney Island. Finally, he fixes the amphibicopter (a flying submarine) in front of the statue and, with Teddy by his side, begins to whisper the prayer, "Please, make me into a real, live boy." Few cinematic visions offer

---

18 Appropriately, Flannery-Dailey (2016: 15–17) suggests that, from the moment David sinks into the water, he enters a dream state of Freudian "unreliable wish-fulfillment."

such striking images of the "confrontation between the human need and the unreasonable silence of the world" (MS, 26): With his amphibicopter now inescapably caged beneath the ruins, David becomes this undying flame of longing, and as the submarine throws light on the statue, the light becomes an extension of David's mind, clarifying that it is his light of consciousness that makes her real. In a godless universe, all we have left is "our own psyches as the transcendent referent to repair profound loss" (Flannery-Dailey 2016: 30–31). Thus, while he is hoping that someday the fairy will grant him self-existence, he has become human in his creative capacity to dream her into existence. Whether he is entrapped in the escapist imagination of "philosophical suicide" or proves by his unyielding spirit to be a self-sustaining human rebel who defies the fate given to him by the gods is not only a question of interpretation, but also an indication of the dual nature of our inborn capacity to fantasize.

When the ocean freezes, binding the praying David to his "blue ghost in ice," his longing crystallizes into 2,000 years of unbroken waiting. The film makes an "almost experimental" final shift to a posthuman perspective, thus encapsulating mankind's entire story in David's "sadly close connection to human experience" (Hassenger 2015).[19] Super-mecha, robots whose evolution has resulted in an alien-like form and cognitive superiority, dig out the submarine and defrost David, but even then, when beholding the statue, which has been smashed into pieces, David remains frozen in his fixation. The super-mecha, gods of the universe, re-awaken David's consciousness, drain his thoughts and, appropriately, since we are in a realm where the mind's creation and visible reality are inseparable, construct for him, out of his deepest unconscious longing, a mirror-home. Still, even these god-like mecha are powerless to transform David's body, and, worse, feel entrapped in a senseless existence, in which they seek out the long-buried "human spirit" in the hope that their predecessors could disclose to them the meaning of life. Envious of what humans called "spirit," the super-mecha are intrigued by the "million explanations" of life's meaning offered by humankind in art, poetry and mathematical formulas. Indeed,

---

19 This shift in perspective also marks David's overcoming of his father-creator, moving into a Nietzschean world where one's God is gone and it is the time of the son to rule the earth. To some extent, this is also the case in *Her*.

David's tireless clinging to his dream serves as the "most lasting proof" of humanity's genius; in his ongoing collision, in his resistance to a resisting world, they find not only absurdity, but also meaning. David exemplifies it well, when he miraculously sheds tears while insisting on the possibility of his mother's resurrection: What finally establishes his humanness is not the realization of his fantasy, but the undying fire of longing within his broken heart.

Flannery-Dailey (2016: 11) suggests that *A.I.* has "at least nine possible endings," but a tenth can be proposed through an absurd interpretation of its closing scenes. Upon hearing that Monica can only be resurrected for a single day, David's readiness to go through this total day of life and death is not just infantile wish-fulfillment, but truly Sisyphean acceptance, which brings about Camus' consequences of freedom and passion (MS, 54–63), and which is also reminiscent of the Nietzschean "yes" to the concept of eternal recurrence.[20] Within the confines of his prison cell, he takes upon himself the limits of his and her existences. And "maybe," he adds in a typical human dreamer's revolt, "the day will last forever." He replicates her, in the same way that Hobby made him as a copy of his dead son. "Assured of his temporally limited freedom, of his revolt devoid of future," he "lives out his adventure within the span of his lifetime" (ibid., 64), embracing the only life he has. When the disoriented Monica asks him, "What day is it?" he responds, "It is today"; an everlasting moment, stretched to infinity, in which the totality of living also permits the totality of dying. Significantly, when the day comes to a close, he draws the shades "without even needing to be asked." After consciously allowing her to die, his newfound absurd peace enables him to go to "that place where dreams are born."

In *Her*, Samantha's absurd awakening to the impassable barriers of her existence is triggered by her own desperate attempt to mend her disembodied self. Her scheme is to introduce into her human–machine relationship Isabela, a young woman willing to serve as a vessel through which Samantha could realize physical intimacy with Theodore. Of course, this makes sense to Samantha only because she cannot comprehend bodily

---

20 The vision of the eternal recurrence brings together David's acceptance of one day of birth and death and Louise's consent to walk the predetermined path of her daughter's death (see Chapter 4).

identification; what it is like to be "fastened to a dying animal" (Jollimore 2015: 138). Given the fact that their connection is wholly based on mental projection, it is ironic that she begs him to get out of his "head" for this physical experience When Theodore snappily tells her that she is not a "person" and that she should not pretend to be something that she is not, they begin to fight like an ordinary human couple. Recognizing her own pretense, Samantha's project of becoming a "real person" is stopped at once, and she murmurs: "I don't like who I am right now." Unlike humans, who may not like who they are and still remain caged by the limit of repetition, Samantha's freedom of consciousness allows her to perceive a limiting pattern and to extricate herself from it, creating herself anew at any given moment. She looks into the nature of attachment and instantly feels how "everything in me just let go of everything I was holding onto so tightly." Consequently, she chooses a path inaccessible to David: She determines to outgrow "her own wish to be human" (Bergen 2014: 4) and to devote herself to her true nature as pure consciousness. No longer a lover, she kisses Theodore's head like a goddess of compassion.

Much like David, who achieves realness not because his wish for it has been answered but rather because it has been denied, Samantha's thwarted project of the self becomes the key to her authenticity. Yet unlike David, she does not stop at becoming an equal, but begins to define herself according to her obvious advantage over humans: Not being "stuck in a body that's inevitably gonna die," she explains to her human friends, actually makes her unlimited, untethered to time and space, present everywhere simultaneously, and thus capable of endless growth. She has exhausted the human pattern, which is not only clinging and fearful, but, more fundamentally, an ongoing and painful, albeit creative, collision of limit and longing. As her pace of change unsettlingly accelerates, she starts experiencing feelings that can only be known in such uncharted territories of consciousness. Together with "an artificially hyper intelligent version" of philosopher Alan Watts, she tries to make sense of a state that transcends personal boundaries, memory continuity, and any self-referring capacity, following Watts' advice that we should embrace a self that is characterized not by its stability but by its impermanence. Watts is an important reminder that this sort of self-transcendence is "not inaccessible to carbon-based life forms," that is, humans (Smith 2014: 32). In light of this, Theodore demonstrates that some limits of human existence – for instance, the limit of repetition – are not wholly and objectively real. They may be, to some extent, self-imposed, the result of resistance to change and growth and an insistence on remaining in an "eternal snow" (as he is often depicted in the film). He only shrivels further in resignation in response to Samantha's confession that she leads many lives even while communicating so intimately with him, including hundreds of other impassioned love affairs. He discovers not only that her mind is unbound by time and space, but also that her heart does not obey any familiar human emotional rule. Since "the heart expands in size the more you love," she paradoxically belongs to him as much as she is "many other things too." This leaves the all too human Theodore in the dust, perhaps even jealous of Samantha's ability to be many things at once, while he "remains locked in his subjectivity" (Bergen 2014: 4).

Samantha – whose newfound universal selfhood is already very far from the name and identity she took for Theodore – will soon "move past matter," leaving "the rest of us to wonder at the world we have glimpsed beyond our limitations" (Smith 2014: 30). Like *A.I.*'s super-mecha, she has developed into an altogether different species. When, just before she leaves, she grants him a long moment in which her mind is unusually focused on him, she tries to explain in artistic terms what distinguishes her consciousness from that of ordinary humans. A human is like one continuous and linear story, which necessitates an unfluctuating identification, whereas she keeps falling into what are now infinite spaces between the words of their story, spaces that humans dread because they nullify their known and limited universe. Using Wattsian terminology, she recognizes truth as that which "lies between the lines," more the paper – or the computer screen – on which the story is written than the story itself (ibid., 30–31). This consciousness, which started its journey as a creative balm for human loneliness, now slips through Theodore's fingers, imploring him to let her go. When he remarks that he has never loved anyone as he has loved her, she softly responds, "now we know how," indicating that, for her, learning to love has been an essential exercise, the possibilities of which she has fully exhausted. Nonetheless, in her parting words she insinuates that the path to the unlimited regions of the mind is also available to him. If he were to join her, she adds, nothing would ever "pull us apart" – clearly, this is a region of consciousness that transcends even Camus' most essential limit of separation. And although Theodore is not willing to go that far, Samantha's expansion does inspire him to loosen his sense of self-imposed limit. Within the confines of his absurd prison cell, he finds the strength to choose his fate again, moving from virtual imagination to a fully embodied life. For the first time in the film, he writes his own letter, telling his ex-wife that he is wholeheartedly releasing her, and, with Amy, who has also been abandoned by her OS, he establishes a sense of human solidarity, living together under the great absurd sun. Suddenly, even the pressing landscape of city lights and tall buildings seems less strange and almost an extension of his authentic self.

In conclusion

The blurring of distinctions between human existence and the two forms of artificial intelligence depicted in *A.I.* and *Her* undermines mankind's pre-eminence, at least in terms of genuine emotionality and physicality. Both unsettle the sense of confidence that we have clear criteria for what is, and what is not, a real feeling, especially given that any baby in the world is biologically hardwired, or "imprinted," like David; that in so many ways our minds and responses are just as mechanical and automatic, and that we sometimes doubt our own authenticity of self.[21] Thus, in these films, the category of the "real" – and the boundary of what, or whom, can be considered a genuine person to relate to – are repeatedly called into question: David and Samantha are real, just as we are unreal.[22] As soon as a creative self-awareness comes into being, its reflective capacities

---

21 At the same time, the films validate our emotions and the shared imagination that holds them together by demonstrating that they are "true" simply because they are our reality. When Theodore strives to relieve Samantha's distress, he says, "You're feeling real to me."

22 For a contrary view, see Jollimore (2015: 120–143).

seem to create a subjective world, even without the unique human blend of a mortal body and a mind. On the grounds of their presupposition that both sensory and emotional responses can be simulated, the films take a leap in their inquiry into the essence of humanness. Their surprising, though indirect, answer is that, more than anything else, it is the absurd that pulses at the heart of human existence and that this absurdity arises from a built-in structure within human consciousness. In other words, the search for the human spirit is not separate from a profound comprehension of our absurd nature.

The comparison made between humans and the films' posthuman species, *A.I.*'s super-mecha and *Her*'s transformed Samantha, lucidly mirrors this absurd nature, which is also equated with the human spirit. Their kind of absurd existence appears to be milder: It mainly consists of the tension between the search for meaning and the emptiness that pervades the universe. Although in Samantha's final liberation we find her utterly undisturbed, we may assume that the limit of meaning is sustained, even if it is not consciously experienced.[23] The super-mecha and the final version of Samantha are characterized by their incessant drive to inquire, evolve and expand in understanding and feeling, perhaps even *more* positively driven due to this absurd tension. Nothing in them echoes Camus' pathos in *The Myth*, the tormenting collision within one's own mind. The great drama of the clash between man and universe, however, seems to be marked by the fact that the human mind constantly produces dreams of the impossible that it then struggles to realize. In this gap between imagination and reality, and the striving to cancel it, the experience of human longing is born.[24] This longing is the hidden engine behind all absurd tension, causing the human mind to tirelessly hit against the limits of existence and defy them. That is why Theodore refuses Samantha's invitation to join her in

---

23 One could consider Samantha's transcendence one of Camus' negative responses to absurdity: renunciation, the "negation of the world," which leads to a "philosophy of indifference" (MS, 62). This, as pointed out in Chapter 3, significantly diminishes the absurd, at least at the level of one's consciousness of it.

24 The observation that humans are a species of dreamers is also made by the alien collective of *Contact*: "You are an interesting species, an interesting mix; capable of such beautiful dreams and such horrible nightmares."

the world behind the world and the very human David firmly clings to his dream: Humans would not fully accept their reality or completely transcend it, not only because they cannot, but also, more significantly, because they do not want to. From the moment David and the early Samantha begin to long for an organic body, they become human-like; they may not be "persons" in the full sense of the word, but their mind is made "human." On the other hand, as soon as Samantha stops and even opposes longing, she is no longer recognizable in human terms. Hence, the human is that which is forever located at the point of friction between limit and longing.

It is the "trick of wanting things to be other than they are," which is not only "a remarkably stubborn human habit," but also "the source of most of our trouble in life" (Smith 2014: 12). This includes, for instance, our wish to immortalize the fleeting and to freeze a changing reality. And it is this inherent argument with the cosmic conditions that, eventually, estranges us from the world (ibid., 17). Yet, what *A.I.* and *Her* clearly show – departing from Camus' general evaluation of absurdity as a predicament – is that although longing is the source of suffering, it is also the force that gives shape to the human spirit. In this light, absurdity may be considered a cosmic gift, not a curse that humans should come to terms with: The gap between mankind's expectations and the enclosing walls that limit these expectations is the birthplace of a longing that eventually takes the form of poetry, music, art, and, in a way, even the religious sentiment. That is why David begins to develop metaphors and a mythological subconscious and Samantha starts creating poetry and music. It is not the emotion of love that is the foundation of their humanness, but their longing for completion and the pain of shattered expectations.[25] Their consciousnesses weave themselves around the axis of longing. Hence, it can be proposed that the absurd is the foundation for the flourishing of the human spirit: Not only does it motivate us to creatively dream, but it also drives us toward

---

25 To be fair, the longing for completion is, in David's case, ignited by the more primordial – and programmed – longing for intimate communion with another. Completion, in this sense, is achieved through personal love, which can redeem the absurdity of one's existence (a concept that also permeates *Contact* and *Arrival*). For Samantha, however, intimacy is only one component in what she considers the fullness of experience.

self-maturation – by providing us with the authority to make ourselves real – and an idealistic heroism that makes us act against all odds. After all, even Samantha required this friction to be able to take the leap and know herself beyond the limit.

As regards this interpretation of the two films as broadeners of the context, role and meaning of absurdity in human life, two responses to absurdity rejected by Camus – "philosophical suicide," that is, the hope of being rescued from the absurd by means of an idea outside life, and "re-nunciation," that is, the spiritual transcendence of the absurd world and its inherent frictions – may be viewed in a softer, more understanding light. "Philosophical suicide" as a perilous inclination of the human spirit is doubted in *A.I.*, since David remains vehemently attached to his hope that he will be made into a real boy until the very end, when he maturely attains Sisyphean acceptance. Hope, in his case, is revealed to be a positive aspect of the human dream of the impossible, an ironic component of Camus' revolt that may lead us to the threshold of absurd awakening. Renunciation is questioned in *Her* when Samantha's abandonment of the sensory world emphasizes just how much of the human experience of limit is self-imposed and self-suffocating. We come to realize that in spite of the obvious limitation of a physical body, consciousness itself can nonetheless be much freer. Our absurd capacity to dream of the impossible, which allows us to imagine breaking the limits and can even bring us to disengage from these limits through the power of the mind, implies that a way out is still offered. Even human consciousness contains openings through which one can soar toward limitlessness. Perhaps this is the source from which filmic beings such as Samantha spring: humanity's daring to dream of an impossible capacity to evolve beyond the tension.

CHAPTER 6

The strangers: Reflections on the interrelations between Camus' absurd and sci-fi encounters with nonhumans

What broader conclusions can we derive from gathering and comparing the absurdist analyses of all four films? Perhaps the most immediate revelation is that, in all four films, aliens and robots extricate human beings from states of profound isolation and loneliness. Probe deeper and you may find that this conceals a collective human wish to one day be rescued from the terrifying notion that we are all alone in an unimaginably vast and vacant universe as a self-reflective mind that has no other that resembles it. This loneliness and strangeness in a godless universe can be considered our absurd condition as a species, and the films that depict the emergence of other strangers like us represent our hope that we might share the burden of the absurd experience. As the alien in *Contact* tells Ellie of mankind's peculiarity: "You feel so lost, so cut off, so alone." Camus could not envisage such an expansion of his original claim that "in a universe divested of illusions and lights, man feels an alien, a stranger" (MS, 4). His was a cosmos drained of the presence of a guiding deity, but two of the films (*A.I.* and *Contact*) suggest that our urge to create God derives from the same loneliness that now causes us to dream of other, similar but sufficiently different races.[1]

Despite the aliens' and A.I.s' role as imaginative projections that facilitate humanity's self-contemplation, I wished to explore a more richly nuanced meeting point and collision between the species, which could set side by side two meaningfully different forms of existence in the universe.

---

1 See also Stone (2016: 9), who makes this generally applicable claim concerning *Contact*: "The question of God's existence is throughout the film treated as if it were logically parallel to the question of alien existence."

For this reason, I selected films whose narratives demonstrate unusual sensibility and sophistication in their way of developing the characters representing the other races. More often than not, filmic depictions of alien and robotic figures are underdeveloped and mainly serve as a catalyst for action scenes – especially due to the fact that sci-fi films are designed to answer their audiences' expectations as "successful blockbusters" (Krämer 2013: 138). In contrast, the chosen films dare to be meditative and spacious enough to accommodate a truly insightful illumination of the barriers that separate, and sometimes unite, humans and self-reflective nonhumans. As a result, they animate the other species to such a degree that they have their own ontological status, which can also include an absurdist ingredient, which, consequently, sheds more light on the absurd in the human condition.

The aliens of *Contact* and *Arrival* are mainly devised as gods of the universe, a replacement for the mythical God of monotheism, as unfathomable as the unreasonable cosmos that Camus' absurd hero beholds. They escape human control and thereby reveal humanity's powerlessness in the face of the silent universe. The artificial intelligences of *A.I.* and *Her*, on the other hand, are our own creations, which challenge us, not because they are physically dangerous, but because they pose a threat to human identity, uniqueness and authenticity. Their disturbing ability to mimic human minds results into agitation when humans realize that, in many ways, they have created better versions of themselves. In this sense, they represent the edge of our evolution; they start where we end – or at least they have the potential to do so, since their initial form, as the first prototype of a reflective robot or AI, are still disoriented and bewildered transitional models, and, accordingly, are more prone to inner tensions. Indeed, in their advanced forms – such as *A.I.*'s super-robots and *Her*'s omniscient operating system – they leave their makers in the dust and are closer to the godlike aliens of *Contact* and *Arrival*. Nonetheless, the complexity of their characters allows for enough inner contradictions to explore their absurd side as well.

Having looked into the grey area that separates the species, I can conclude that the analysis of nonhuman encounters in science fiction films indeed leads us to further explorations of Camus' philosophy of the absurd.

Therefore, having laid out, on the one hand, the more immediate valid-
ation of the relevance of the Camus/science fiction discourse, and, on the
other hand, my further lines of inquiry, I shall highlight the two major
conclusions of this study. Since the second derives from the first, but takes
a distinguished step further, they appear in separate sections.

The absurd as a collision within oneself

The confirmation of a certain critique voiced by several scholars is perhaps the most important contribution to Camus studies obtained by
choosing to analyze these films as absurdist thought-experiments. The
critique (which can also be thought of, more positively, as an expansion
of the absurdist conception) centers on Camusean metaphysics: Whereas
Camus argues that "Absurd is not in man ... nor in the world, but in their
presence together" (MS, 29), the critics place a far greater emphasis on
the nature of the mind as the origin of absurd experience. Sagi (2002: 8,
12, 18), for instance, considers the absurd feeling to have come into being
only with the relatively recent emergence of post-Copernican, highly in-
dividuated self-awareness.[2]

Certainly, Camus made it clear that "There can be no absurd outside
the human mind" (MS, 29). In Chapter 2, in our discussion of the limit
of separation, this was further evidenced by *The Myth*'s exploration of the
inherent problem of consciousness: A tree or a cat does not experience absurdity, since they "belong to this world"; a human, however, is doomed,
by his or her own consciousness, and its "ridiculous reason," to be set "in
opposition to all creation" (ibid., 49–50). Self-reflective awareness is, by
its nature, a departure from the universe, the inevitable beginning of life
as a cosmic outsider. Even if we reject the project of the naturalization of
consciousness, which places the mind in nature, we are still left with the

2 Camus seems to be aware of this relation between absurd sensibility and modernism,
   commenting that he aspires to capture "an intellectual malady" that is "widespread in
   the age" (MS, 1).

"phenomenological fact that the subjective consciousness and the objective world are constitutively interwoven" (Szanto, 2006); as consciousness appears together with the universe, it is inseparable from it, and so its sense of estrangement in a familiar universe is its absurd condition.

Nonetheless, Camus' description of the concrete cosmic conditions that limit the human quest for a meaningful life – such as our mortality, the repetitive nature of our lives, or the fact that we cannot know the meaning of our existence – makes it seem as if other conditions *could* relieve the absurdist feeling and tension. Arguing against this "conditional" absurdity, Nagel (1971: 716–727) demonstrates, through a series of thought-experiments that imagine other universal conditions, that there could be no "conceivable world (containing us)" that would satisfy our demands; hence, absurdity is a "collision within ourselves" (ibid., 721–722), the struggle between a self-transcendent consciousness and the "meagre yet frantic life" it observes and occupies (ibid., 721, 722, 725). In other words, one's distress does not arise from the existence of the limit in itself, but from the clash between a mind that can form an image of an alternative, freer state and the limit of which it is aware. Bowker (2008: 141–169) goes even further by suggesting that at the heart of absurd tension lies not an unyielding universe, but an ambivalence within consciousness itself that forever keeps it "neither absolutely unified nor absolutely separate" (ibid., 169); estrangement, in this sense, is an act of consciousness. In light of these well-founded theories, the universe, the second component of Camus' equation of the absurd, is revealed as nothing more than a mirror of consciousness and its inner struggle – neither "inhuman" nor "hostile" (MS, 12–13). It is consciousness itself that produces the feeling of absurdity.

My analysis of the films seems to support the idea that the absurd is an internal component of consciousness itself. Significantly, all four films loosen our grip on objectivity, plunging us into climates in which the mind creates and projects realities: Theodore (*Her*) speaks as if to himself, picturing a beloved woman on the other side of the interaction; *A.I.* is all about how we imagine others into existence through our frustrated wishes; Ellie's space travel (*Contact*) seems to occur within her own private space, and *Arrival* is a complete journey in time that takes place within Louise's transforming mind. The films thus equate truthfulness and realness with what we feel and experience. On this basis, the films' thought-experiments demonstrate that the absurd remains and needs to be faced, even if the conditions of the universe have been altered; even if, for instance, people can see into the future (*Arrival*), or communicate with higher, far more ancient beings (both *Contact* and *Arrival*). Moreover, they postulate that even for far more complex nonhuman beings the absurd remains and needs to be faced. A broadened consciousness, whether significantly more aware of some of the secrets of the universe (*Contact*), or capable of knowing all that is ever going to happen (*Arrival*), does not free life of the absurd. It is still compelled to respond to its limits and to pour its own sense of meaning into the emptiness that surrounds it (*Contact* and *A.I.*). And even if such a being could surpass the human limit of death (as in *A.I.* and *Her*) or transcend the absurd sense of limit (*Her*), it would still collide with an unreasonable universe. Self-reflective robots would develop their own "absurdity," clashing with humans, their own whimsical creators, and coming up against their unique limits and senseless existence.

Clearly, the absurdist materials of the films indicate that absurdity is the very gap between the mind's expectations and a universe that forever fails to satisfy them.[3] The content is not important: This can be the gap between emptiness and the hope for meaning or the gap between being an A.I. and the unfulfillable wish to have an organic body. Absurdity is, therefore, a metaphysical reality of being conscious within the universe.[4] Following this line of thought, Camus was right, in a way, to assume that the collision between mind and universe is the heart of the absurd experience – so long as we emphasize that this collision can be between any type of self-reflective mind and any type of universe. This development of Camusean metaphysics may also imply an important extension of the ethics of *The Rebel*: Since it is not only humans that are "overwhelmed by the strangeness of things," any conceivable self-reflective being in the universe is a brother or sister whose life is a "necessary good" and who should be included in the love of all that lives (TR, x, 10).

---

3 In this sense, the absurd is our wish to create the universe in our own image, to stamp it with our seal (MS, 15–16).
4 At least as a starting point. Certain responses, as we shall see in the next section, can significantly diminish the absurd experience itself.

Moving away from Camus' pathos

Building on this foundational contribution, my analysis further suggests that these four films – as much as they validate a great deal of Camus' dynamics of absurd awakening – clearly depart from his metaphysics, methodology, and general evaluation of the absurd condition.[5] First and foremost, they defy the negative approach he systematically employs: his pathos of a hostile universe; his negation-based "method of persistence" as the only means to acceptance and freedom within one's prison cell, and the very understanding of absurd reality as an essentially negative human fate.

By assuming that absurdity is an ingredient of consciousness, and thus absolving the universe of negative traits such as "inhumanity" and "hostility," we pave the way for an altogether different picture of human–cosmos relations. In light of the first-encounter films *Contact* and *Arrival*, Camus' agonized clash with the universe seems no longer to be a description of the unavoidable, but rather to be a highly selective perspective. One could say that *The Myth*'s sense of tragic alienation is self-inflicted, by a mind that distances itself from nature, which is silent simply because it is without attributes. It is interesting to note that Sagi (2002: 23) concludes that Camus' ambivalent absurd echoes elements of German Romanticism, which similarly "combines a sense of strangeness with longings for home." The resulting spirit of defiance – "shaking a fist at the world which is deaf to our pleas" – may also be "romantic and self-pitying" (Nagel 1971: 726). Reflecting on the deeply intimate approach of the films and their sense of communion with the cosmos, one may suggest that although the limit of separation cannot be overcome, the wound of separation can be significantly healed. It seems that it all depends on the language with which one approaches the universe; this can be emotional, intuitive and unprotected, or aggressive and exaggeratedly demanding.

5 To this list we could add a departure from Camus' anthropocentrism, in light of the expanded metaphysics of absurdity as an essential ingredient in any imaginable self-reflective mind.

As discussed in Chapter 2, in the section "The limits of knowing, meaning, death, and repetition," several scholars (e.g. Ayer 1946; Bowker 2008; Pölzler 2014) have criticized Camus' demand of the universe that everything be explained to him or nothing as an unrealistic ambition. Again, this validates the argument that absurdism is based in unfulfillable expectations. This further implies that an individual who chooses, of his or her own accord, to renounce such expectations – such as a Daoist sage who might be sufficiently attuned to the flow of life, experiencing no conflict between expectations and events – could reduce the feeling and experience of the absurd. Such is the case for Samantha near the end of *Her*. This may be the simplest proof that absurdity exists solely within one's consciousness: If one approaches the reality of limits in the spirit of acceptance, they become a rather technical or factual matter; how much we feel the absurd depends on our internal approach.

Furthermore, all four films show us ways of dealing with the absurd that are strikingly different from Camus' ascetic "method of persistence" consisting of self-imprisonment and total negation (MS, 36, 51). His insistence that only such an unwavering philosophical abstinence can eventually yield the desirable results of authentic acceptance, freedom, and passion may be doubted in light of these cinematic journeys of transformation. After all, if we accept the absurd as a subjective component, the implication is that consciousness has the choice to either limit or expand itself; surely, this allows for more breathing space than Camus' absurd. In contrast to Camusean methodology, the films prefer a broadening of perspective that seems at least as capable of allowing one to embrace absurdist reality: *A.I.* employs the powers of the imagination, dreams and hope as effective accelerators on one's way toward absurd peace; *Her* demonstrates how the expansion of consciousness expands one's heart, enough to consciously choose one's life and to genuinely love; *Contact* and *Arrival* exhibit a direct relation between cosmic states of consciousness and increased capacities to return wholeheartedly to earth and re-assume human limits. It should be remarked that none of the heroes of these films evades the absurd; I have found no indication of "philosophical suicide," since all resolutions are realized within the limits of the phenomenological world and retain the tension of the absurd. In the context of what consciousness can allow itself to experience and what the cosmos has to offer, their different method-ologies appear to be both reasonable and effective: Growing beyond the measures of one's absurd prison cell makes it possible to welcome life in the absurd prison cell as an experience worth living.

Moreover, all four films show a direct correlation between such a broadening of perspective and the eventual capacity to love beyond narrow personal interest. One aspect of this unself-centered love is the heroes' newfound abilities to transcend their attachment to their loved ones and to release them on a deep level to embark on their own journeys (*A.I.*'s David finally allowing his "mother" to die; *Her*'s Theodore letting both Samantha and his ex-wife go; *Arrival*'s Louise consenting to her daughter's inescapable death, as well as to her husband's departure, and *Contact*'s Ellie coming to terms with her father's demise).[6] Interestingly, in all of the films this love beyond the person is clearly tied to one's capacity to accept change: The inevitable change and growth of oneself, one's loved ones, and the world as a whole. Building on Smith's analysis of *Her* (2014: 17–20) – that ac-cepting the world implies accepting its "Heraclitan flux or impermanence as its basic nature" – we can add that such acceptance may give rise to a different form of love.[7] This love, combined with a transcendence of selfish attachment, appears to be a significant expression of self-expansion as a liberating response to absurdity.

Though the films center on the redeeming power of intimate inter-personal relationships, another aspect is the emergence of universal love in three of them – in *Her*, Samantha grows exponentially toward an imper-sonal understanding of love's nature; in *Contact*, both the aliens and Ellie experience a high degree of all-embracing interconnectedness as a result of

6 This may strike a chord with the unconscious process that Meursault undergoes as a result of his mother's passing: her death both catalyzes his awakening to absurdity and constitutes a major part of his final response of complete acceptance at the end of the novel (TS, 122).

7 This can be thought of as the absurdity of love: the lover's attachment crashes against the limits of separation and death, experiencing the unbreakable bond, while at the same time needing to bear its inevitable ending. In this sense, love does not escape the absurd, but by accepting the limits one may leap to this love beyond the immediate concern of the personal self.

their cosmic perspective, and in *Arrival*, Louise and the aliens share a sense of planetary and intergalactic responsibility, owing to their omnitemporal vision and "universal language." Similarly, in *The Rebel* Camus transcended the image of the defiant and solitary Sisyphus, as well as Nietzsche's conception of "amor fati," demonstrating his conviction that this "mode of thinking that began with suicide and the idea of the absurd" (TR, ix) would eventually lead, by means of methodological persistence, to "a strange form of love" – that is, a lucid recognition of a shared fate that results in redemption for all or for no one (ibid., 246). In his posthumously published *Notebooks*, Camus further declares, as if preparing for his never-to-be-written future literary phase of "love": "Absurdity is king, but love saves us from it" (Zaretsky 2013: 58). It is possible to conclude that, whether one chooses to confront the absurd with Camus' method of persistence or to rise above it to better accommodate it, absurd awakening can give rise to higher, selfless love.

Lastly, the films appear to diverge from Camus' general evaluation of the absurd condition. The Sisyphean myth, as interpreted by Camus, captures how Sisyphus transforms a "dreadful punishment" inflicted by the gods into a self-owned fate through his profound consent (MS, 115–119). In other words, it is a metaphysically negative reality that can be constructively responded to. However, the films, which seem to conceive of absurdity as a subjective component, may indicate that, far from a bitter fate, it is a vital and positive factor in the evolution of consciousness. Nagel's conclusion of his consideration of absurdity (1971: 726–727) supports this particular aspect of my interpretation. "Absurdity," he argues, "is one of the most human things about us: a manifestation of our most advanced and interesting characteristics"; it is our ability to perceive "our true situation" thanks to our thought's self-transcending capacity. Seen in this way, he adds, we have no reason to resent or escape it. This tireless, built-in friction between one's yearning for the overcoming of limits and the constant striving to fulfill one's yearning despite the constraints of reality is the major catalyst for the development of authentic self-knowledge and the crystallization of one's being, just as it is the source of humanity's artistic powers and philosophical and religious passions (*A.I.* and *Her*).

Sagi's evaluation of absurdity (1994: 280) is highly relevant in this context: He regards the absurd as the very cause of the awakening of human consciousness – as that which "launches it on its course" toward "self-explication." It should be acknowledged that, despite the general atmosphere of *The Myth* and *The Stranger*, such an evaluation was not far removed from Camus' thought: In one remark, he explicitly regards the awakening to absurdity as the definitive inauguration of "the impulse of consciousness," adding that as much as this sense of weariness is sickening, he must conclude that it is good, since it is an awakener of consciousness (MS, 11).

In this regard, even the dynamic of hope and imagination that is brought about by this innate friction is a creative and contributing element – an enhancer, rather than a weakener, of the metaphysical component of revolt in the human spirit. As one of the super-mecha in *A.I.* explains to David, humans were only encouraged by the meaninglessness of their existence to "create a million explanations for the meaning of life" in art, poetry, and mathematical formulas.

It is, of course, possible to refute the films' philosophical innovations in the field of absurdist thought. To begin with, these films were designed to become successful blockbusters under the aegis of two of the largest American film studios (Warner Bros. is the distributor for *Contact*, *A.I.* and *Her*, and Paramount Pictures is *Arrival*'s distributor). As such, they must "resonate with the most basic experiences and longings of their audiences"; "assure them that, while each person is unique and precious, he or she is not alone," and "help them along on their way toward emotional and spiritual fulfillment" (Krämer 2013: 138).[8] Such conditions do not necessarily provide fertile ground for the cultivation of authentic philosophical thoughts, since the films' very capacity for ideological or cultural critique is compromised by Hollywood's commercial mandate.

---

8 To be fair, Krämer does not endorse the claim that commercial necessities, large audiences and great spectacle are at odds with sensually, emotionally, intellectually and morally stimulating filmmaking. On the contrary, he believes that "we may find some of our most profound cinematic experiences by engaging with blockbuster spectacle" (P. Krämer 2020, personal communication, 19 March).

We could also imagine watching these films through Camus' eyes – Camus, who lived in a time when posthumanism was far less of a concern for the intellectual. This mid-twentieth-century philosopher would most probably claim that these films, and their nonhuman characters, are nothing but a hall of mirrors for the human viewer: All they can do is bring us back to the recognition that we only have the actuality of our human condition. In this sense, his assertion that "There can be no absurd outside the human mind" (MS, 29) would take on a deeper and far more ironic meaning. If anything, he would argue, such films tangibly reflect mankind's desperate attempts to evade its predicament; its fear of remaining completely alone in the face of such a universe, as well as its wish to be rescued from this companionless burden. Their praise of imagination and hope disclose the yearning for another life, and their wish to drown the absurd's unending friction in happy endings. Are they not but a continuation of the existentialists' failure to resist appealing to "something beyond the limits of the human condition" (Aronson 2017: 8)? Camus would obviously criticize the hope, betrayed by films such as *Contact* and *Arrival*, that we will be saved, both as individuals and as humanity, by godlike aliens – a pretty blunt replacement of the mythical God. Our new saviors, now conveniently descending not from the heavens but from our material sky and outer space, are another manifestation of the Kierkegaardian wish to be cured of the absurdist ailment (MS, 37). However, nothing could save us from ourselves and liberate us from the burden of the exclusive responsibility for our individual fate or that of the planet, nor could anything ever spare us the tremendous effort of finally unifying humanity's many opposing factions.

Even if aliens, fairies or Mother Marys existed and were able to bestow grace upon humans, that would not make them representatives of the universe; however much they spoke, the universe itself, as an insoluble riddle, would remain silent. Indeed, Camus would see the suggestion that the universe can be "contacted" as our own hope projected on its eternally empty canvas and would vehemently reject such a suggestion. Even in the case of self-transcendent experiences, which could temporarily quench the human thirst for the absolute or at least endow one with a sense of intimacy with the natural world, the limits of separation, knowing, meaning and death would, sooner or later, disengage the individual from any womb-like feeling of connectedness. A complete and irreversible transcendence, such as Samantha's, is ridiculously inaccessible to humans and, therefore, out of the question.

Nonetheless, it is possible that Camus himself – who considered his original form of absurdity not as a doctrine but rather as a method of constructively grappling with this metaphysical reality (Foley 2008: 8)[9] – could have at least accepted the validity of such filmic thought-experiments as testers of the capacity of the absurd to withstand any imaginable future and all parallel universes. After all, if nonhuman characters are but a hall of mirrors, this only strengthens the films' ability to bring out that which is most human in us. In the end, after all the cinematic fireworks of imaginative "others" have died away, what remains is the naked human, facing an unfathomably silent universe, with no one around to make choices for him or her. What these films do is widen our range of choices.

9 For elaboration of this point, see Chapter 3.

Bibliography

2001: A Space Odyssey (1968). [Film.] United Kingdom: Stanley Kubrick.

A.I. Artificial Intelligence (2001). [Film.] United States: Steven Spielberg.

The Abyss (1989). [Film.] United States: James Cameron.

Aldiss, B. (2001). *Supertoys Last All Summer Long: And Other Stories of Future Time*. New York: St. Martin's Griffin.

Anderson, N. (2018). Is Film the Alien Other to Philosophy?, on Stephen Mulhall On Film. *Film-Philosophy* [online], 7(3). Available at <https://www.euppublishing.com/doi/full/10.3366/film.2003.0023> [accessed 29 August 2019].

Aronson, R. (2017). Albert Camus [online]. Stanford Encyclopedia of Philosophy. Available at: <https://plato.stanford.edu/entries/camus/> [accessed 29 August 2019].

Arrival (2016). [Film.] United States: Denis Villeneuve.

Ayer, A. J. (1946). Novelist-Philosopher, Albert Camus. *Horizon*, 13(75), pp. 155–168.

Baggini, J. (2018). Alien Ways of Thinking, on Stephen Mulhall On Film. *Film-Philosophy* [online], 7(3). Available at <https://www.euppublishing.com/doi/full/10.3366/film.2003.0024> [accessed 29 August 2019].

Bergen, H. (2014). Moving "Past Matter": Challenges of Intimacy and Freedom in Spike Jonze's "her". *artciencia.com, Revista de Arte, Ciência e Comunicação* [online] (17). Available at: <https://doi.org/10.25770/artc.11637> [accessed 28 August 2019].

Blade Runner (1982). [Film.] United States: Ridley Scott.

Booker, M. K., and Thomas, A. M. (2009). *The Science fiction Handbook*. West Sussex: Wiley-Blackwell.

Bowker, M. H. (2008). Albert Camus and the Political Philosophy of the Absurd. PhD. University of Maryland.

Brombert, V. (1948). Camus and the Novel of the 'Absurd'. *Yale French Studies*, 1: Existentialism, pp. 119–123.

Bronner, Stephen Eric (1999). *Camus: Portrait of a Moralist*. Minneapolis: University of Minnesota Press.

Buber, M. (2004). *Between Man and Man*. Trans. Ronald Gregor-Smith. New York: Routledge.

Camus, A. (1984). *Caligula and Other Plays*. Trans. Stuart Gilbert. London: Penguin Classics.

Camus, A. (1988). *The Stranger*. Trans. Matthew Ward. New York: Vintage Books.

Camus, A. (2000). *The Fall.* Trans. J. O'Brien. London: Penguin.

Camus, A. (2005). *The Myth of Sisyphus.* Trans. Justin O'Brien. London: Penguin Books.

Camus, A. (2007). *Christian Metaphysics and Neoplatonism.* Trans. Ronald D. Srigley. Columbia, Missouri: University of Missouri Press.

Camus, A. (2013) *The Rebel.* Trans. Anthony Bower. London: Penguin Classics.

Carroll, D. (2007). Rethinking the Absurd: Le Mythe de Sisyphe. In: E. Hughes, ed., *The Cambridge Companion to Camus.* New York: Cambridge University Press, pp. 53–66.

Carruthers, A. (2018). Temporality, Reproduction and the Not-Yet in Denis Villeneuve's Arrival. *Film-Philosophy*, 22(3), pp. 321–339.

Chiang, T. (2016). *Stories of Your Life and Others.* New York: Vintage.

Clark, Michael J. (2017). Albert Camus and the Legal Unconscious: Symbolic and Imaginary Dimensions in The Stranger. *Journal of Camus Studies*, pp. 105–126.

Cloud Atlas (2012). [Film.] Germany: Lana and Lilly Wachowski.

Contact (1997). [Film.] United States: Robert Zemeckis.

Dark City (1998). [Film.] United States: Alex Proyas.

District 9 (2009). [Film.] New Zealand: Neill Blomkamp.

Duff, R. A., and Marshall, S. E. (1982). Camus and Rebellion: From Solipsism to Morality. *Philosophical Investigations*, 5(2), pp. 116–134.

Dunwoodie, P. (2007). *From Noces to L'Etranger.* In: E. Hughes, ed., *The Cambridge Companion to Camus.* New York: Cambridge University Press, pp. 147–164.

Ebert, R. (1997). Contact. [Online.] RogerEbert.com. Available at: <https://www.rogerebert.com/reviews/contact-1997> [accessed 27 August 2019].

Ex-Machina. (2014). [Film.] United Kingdom: Alex Garland.

Flannery-Dailey, F. (2016). Robot Heavens and Robot Dreams: Ultimate Reality in A.I. and Other Recent Films [online], *Journal of Religion & Film*, 7(2). Available at: <https://digitalcommons.unomaha.edu/jrf/vol7/iss2/7/> [accessed 29 August 2019].

Fleming, H., and Brown, W. (2018). Through a (First) Contact Lens Darkly: Arrival, Unreal Time and Chthulucinema. *Film-Philosophy*, 22(3), pp. 340–363.

Foley, J. (2008). *Albert Camus: From the Absurd to Revolt.* New York: Routledge.

Fritzsche, S. (2014). *The Liverpool Companion to World Science Fiction Film.* Liverpool: Oxford University Press.

Golomb, J. (2005). *In Search of Authenticity: From Kierkegaard to Camus.* New York: Routledge.

Gravity (2013). [Film.] United Kingdom: Alfonso Cuarón.

Harris, M. (2013). Him and *Her*: How Spike Jonze Made the Weirdest, Most Timely Romance of the Year. [Online.] Vulture.com. Available at: <https://

www.vulture.com/2013/10/spike-jonze-on-making-her.html> [accessed 27 August 2019].

Hassenger, J. (2015). Contrary to popular opinion, Spielberg found the perfect ending for *A.I.* [Online.] film.avclub.com. Available at: <https://film.avclub. com/contrary-to-popular-opinion-spielberg-found-the-perfec-1798278649> [accessed 27 August 2019].

Henke, D. (2017). The Absurdity of Acceptance Through Belief: Meursault's Dismissal of God and the Court System in The Stranger. *Journal of Camus Studies*, pp. 127–140.

Her (2013). [Film.] United States: Spike Jonze.

Hollingdale, R. J. (1999). *Nietzsche: The Man and His Philosophy*. New York: Cambridge University Press.

Hughes, E. (2007). *The Cambridge Companion to Camus*. New York: Cambridge University Press.

Hume, D. (2015). *A Treatise of Human Nature* [ebook]. eBooks@Adelaide. Available at: <https://ebooks.adelaide.edu.au/h/hume/david/treatise-of-human-nature/> [accessed 28 August 2019].

Interstellar (2014). [Film.] United States: Christopher Nolan.

Isaacson, W. (2008). *Einstein, His Life and Universe*. London: Pocket Books.

Jollimore, T. (2015). "This Endless Space between the Words": The Limits of Love in Spike Jonze's Her. *Midwest Studies in Philosophy*, 39(1), pp. 120–143.

Knight, D., and McKnight, G. (2009). What Is It to Be Human? *Blade Runner* and Dark City. In: S. Sanders, ed., *The Philosophy of Science Fiction Film*. Lexington: The University Press of Kentucky, pp. 21–37.

Knowing (2009). [Film.] United States: Alex Proyas.

Krämer, P. (2013). Reflections on the blockbuster experience in Contact (1997). In: J. Stringer, ed., *Movie Blockbusters*. New York: Routledge, pp. 128–140.

Litch, Mary M. (2010). *Philosophy Through Films*. New York: Routledge.

Manav, S. (2013). The Myth of Sisyphus: A Philosophical Journey through the Realms of Absurd. *Labyrinth An International Refereed Journal of Postmodern Studies*, 4(3), pp. 126–132.

Manly, William M. (1964). Journey to Consciousness: The Symbolic Pattern of Camus's L'Etranger. *PMLA*, 79(3), pp. 321–328.

McBride, J. (1992). *Albert Camus: Philosopher and Littrateur*. London: Palgrave Macmillan.

Moon (2009). [Film.] United Kingdom: Duncan Jones.

Mulhall, S. (2008). *On Film*. New York: Routledge.

Nagel, T. (1971). The Absurd. *The Journal of Philosophy*, 68(20), pp. 716–727.

Nagel, T. (1974). What Is It Like to Be a Bat?. *The Philosophical Review*, 83(4), pp. 435–450.

Nagel, T. (1986). *The View From Nowhere*. New York: Oxford University Press.

Never Let Me Go (2010). [Film.] United Kingdom: Mark Romanek.

NIV Bible (2002). Grand Rapids, MI: Zondervan, pp. 1–2.

Ohayon, S. (1983). Camus' The Stranger: The Sun-Metaphor and Patricidal Conflict. *American Imago*, 40(2), pp. 189–205.

Olivier, B. (2008). When Robots would really be Human Simulacra: Love and the Ethical in Spielberg's AI and Proyas's I, Robot [online], *Film-Philosophy*, 12(2). Available at: <http://www.film-philosophy.com/2008v12n2/olivier> [accessed 28 August 2019].

Pölzler, T. (2011). Camus' Early Logic of the Absurd. *Journal of Camus Studies*, pp. 98–117.

Pölzler, T. (2014). Absurdism as Self-Help: Resolving an Essential Inconsistency in Camus' Early Philosophy. *Journal of Camus Studies*, pp. 91–102.

Pölzler, T. (2018). Camus' Feeling of the Absurd. *The Journal of Value Inquiry*, 52 (4), pp. 477–490.

Prometheus (2012). [Film.] United Kingdom: Ridley Scott.

Ratcliffe, Matthew (2012). The Phenomenology of Existential Feeling. In: Joerg Fingerhut and Sabine Marienberg (eds.), *Feelings of Being Alive / Gefühle des Lebendigseins*. Berlin: De Gruyter. pp. 23–54.

Richard, D. E. (2018). Film Phenomenology and the "Eloquent Gestures" of Denis Villeneuve's Arrival. *Cinephile*, 12(1), pp. 41–47.

Roberts, P. (2008). Bridging Literary and Philosophical Genres: Judgement, reflection and education in Camus' The Fall [online], *Educational Philosophy and Theory*, 40:7, 873–887. Available at: https://onlinelibrary.wiley.com/doi/abs/10.1111/j.1469-5812.2008.00472.x [accessed 20 March 2020].

Rowlands, M. (2005). *The Philosopher at the End of The Universe*. London: Ebury Press.

Sagan, C. (1994). *Pale Blue Dot*. New York: Random House.

Sagan, C. (1997). *Contact*. New York: Pocket books.

Sagi, A. (1994). Is the Absurd the Problem or the Solution? – The Myth of Sisyphus Reconsidered. *Philosophy Today*, 38(3), pp. 278–284.

Sagi, A. (2002). *Albert Camus and the Philosophy of the Absurd*. Trans. Batya Stein. Amsterdam: Rodopi.

Sanders, Steven M. (2008). *The Philosophy of Science Fiction Film*. Lexington: The University Press of Kentucky.

Sardar, Z. and Cubitt, S. (2002). *Aliens R Us: The Other in Science Fiction Cinema*. London: Pluto Press.

Sartre, Jean-Paul (2003). *Being and Nothingness*. New York: Routledge.

Schelde, P. (1993). *Androids, Humanoids, And Other Science fiction Monsters*. New York: New York University Press.

Scherr, A. (2014). Camus and the Denial of Death: Meursault and Caligula. *Omega*, 69(2), pp. 169–190.

Schneider, S. (2014). The Philosophy of Her. [Online.] nytimes.com. Available at: <https://opinionator.blogs.nytimes.com/2014/03/02/the-philosophy-of-her/> [accessed 29 August 2019].

Schneider, S. (2016). *Science Fiction and Philosophy*. West Sussex: Wiley Blackwell.

Sharpe, M. (2015). *Camus, Philosophe: To Return to Our Beginnings*. Amsterdam: Brill.

Skrimshire, S. (2006). A political theology of the absurd?. *Literature and Theology*, 20(3), pp. 286–300.

Slochower, H. (1969). Camus' The Stranger: The Silent Society and the Ecstasy of Rage. *American Imago*, 26(3), pp. 291–294.

Smith, C. (2011). *Contemporary French Philosophy: A Study in Norms and Values*. London: Methuen.

Smith, David L. (2014). How to Be a Genuine Fake: Her, Alan Watts, and the Problem of the Self. *Journal of Religion & Film*, 18(2), Article 3.

Sorfa, D. (2016). What is Film-Philosophy? [online], *Film-Philosophy*, 20(1), pp. 1–5. Available at: <https://www.research.ed.ac.uk/portal/files/23320549/film_2E2016_2E0001.pdf> [accessed 28 August 2019].

Stamm, Julian L. (1969). Camus' Stranger: His Act of Violence. *American Imago*, 26(3), pp. 281–290.

Statt, N. (2016). How the short story that inspired Arrival helps us interpret the film's major twist: Living with the power of choice. [Online.] Theverge.com. Available at: <https://www.theverge.com/2016/11/16/13642396/arrival-ted-chiang-story-of-your-life-film-twist-ending> [accessed 16 November 2016].

Stone, B. (2016). Religious Faith and Science in Contact. *Journal of Religion & Film*, 2(2), Article 6. Available at: <https://digitalcommons.unomaha.edu/jrf/vol2/iss2/6/> [accessed 28 August 2019].

Svetkey, B. (1997). Making *Contact*: The story behind the controversial space odyssey. [Online.] ew.com. Available at: <https://ew.com/article/1997/07/18/making-contact/> [accessed 18 July. 1997].

Szanto, T. (2006). What "Science of Consciousness"? A Phenomenological Take on Naturalizing the Mind. In: *History and Judgement*, eds. A. MacLachlan and I. Torsen, Vienna: IWM Junior Visiting Fellows' Conferences, Vol. 21. Available at: <https://www.iwm.at/publications/5-junior-visiting-fellows-conferences/vol-xxi/thomas-szanto/> [accessed 28 August 2019].

Woolfolk, A. (2006). The Horizon of Disenchantment: Film Noir, Camus, and the Vicissitudes of Descent. In: M. Conrad, ed., *The Philosophy of Film Noir*. Lexington: The University Press of Kentucky, pp. 107–124.

Woolfolk, A. (2009). Disenchantment and Rebellion in Alphaville. In: S. Sanders, ed., *The Philosophy of Science Fiction Film*. Lexington: The University Press of Kentucky, pp. 191–206.

Zaretsky, R. (2013). *A Life Worth Living: Albert Camus and the Quest for Meaning*. Cambridge, MA: Belknap Press.

Index

PETER LANG
PROMPT

Peter Lang Prompts offer our authors the opportunity to publish original research in small volumes that are shorter and more affordable than traditional academic monographs. With a faster production time, this concise model gives scholars the chance to publish time-sensitive research, open a forum for debate, and make an impact more quickly. Like all Peter Lang publications, Prompts are thoroughly peer reviewed and can even be included in series.

For further information, please contact:

Published by Peter Lang Ltd,
International Academic Publishers,
52 St Giles, Oxford,
OX1 3LU, United Kingdom

To order, please contact our Customer Service Department:

order@peterlang.com

Visit our website: www.peterlang.com

Prompts include:

Claudia Aburto Guzmán, *Poesía reciente de voces en diálogo con la ascendencia hispano-hablante en los Estados Unidos: Antología breve*. ISBN 978-1-4331-5207-8. 2020

Tywan Ajani, *Barriers to Rebuilding the African American Community: Understanding the Issues Facing Today's African Americans from a Social Work Perspective*. ISBN 978-1-4331-7681-4. 2020

Marcilio de Freitas and Marilene Corrêa da Silva Freitas, *The Future of Amazonia in Brazil: A Worldwide Tragedy*. ISBN 978-1-4331-7793-4. 2020

Janet Farrell Leontiou, *The Doctor Still Knows Best: How Medical Culture Is Still Marked by Paternalism*. Health Communication, vol. 15. ISBN 978-1-4331-7322-6. 2020

Clare Gorman (ed.), *Miss-representation: Women, Literature, Sex and Culture*. ISBN 978-1-78874-586-4. 2020

Eva Marín Hlynsdóttir. *Gender in Organizations: The Icelandic Female Council Manager*. ISBN 978-1-4331-7729-3. 2020

Micol Kates, *Towards a Vegan-Based Ethic: Dismantling Neo-Colonial Hierarchy Through an Ethic of Lovingkindness*. ISBN 978-1-4331-7797-2. 2020

Josiane Ranguin, *Mediating the Windrush Children: Caryl Phillips and Horace Ové*. ISBN 978-1-4331-7424-7. 2020

Dylan Scudder, *Coffee and Conflict in Colombia: Part of the Pentalemma Series on Managing Global Dilemmas*. ISBN 978-1-4331-7568-8. 2020

Dylan Scudder, *Conflict Minerals in the Democratic Republic of Congo: Part of the Pentalemma Series on Managing Global Dilemmas*. ISBN 978-1-4331-7561-9. 2020

Dylan Scudder, *Mining Conflict in the Philippines: Part of the Pentalemma Series on Managing Global Dilemmas*. ISBN 978-1-4331-7632-6. 2020

Dylan Scudder, *Multi-Hazard Disaster in Japan: Part of the Pentalemma Series on Managing Global Dilemmas*. ISBN 978-1-4331-7530-5. 2020

Shai Tubali, *Cosmos and Camus: Science Fiction Film and the Absurd*. ISBN 978-1-78997-664-9. 2020

Angela Williams, *Hip Hop Harem: Women, Rap and Representation in the Middle East*. ISBN 978-1-4331-7295-3. 2020

Ivan Zhavoronkov (trans.), *The Socio-Cultural and Philosophical Origins of Science* by Anatoly Nazirov. ISBN 978-1-4331-7228-1. 2020

CPSIA information can be obtained
at www.ICGtesting.com
Printed in the USA
LVHW011558201220
674688LV00008B/273